TRUST ME

The insider's guide
to being the go-to
person at work

TRACY LALONDE

Trust Me
Copyright © 2024 by Tracy LaLonde. All rights reserved.

No part of this publication may be reproduced, stored in a retrieval system
or transmitted in any way by any means, electronic, mechanical, photocopy,
recording or otherwise without the prior permission of the author except
as provided by USA copyright law.

This book is designed to provide accurate and authoritative information
with regard to the subject matter covered.

Cover design by Sherri Konick.
Interior design by DTPerfect Book Design.

Published in the United States of America by James House Media.

Identifiers:
979-8-9915619-0-7 (Paperback)
979-8-9915619-1-4 (E-Book)

CONTENTS

· ·

THE CURRENCY OF TRUST

At its most fundamental level, trust within the workplace acts as an invisible, yet potent, force that shapes interactions, decisions, and outcomes. Legendary investor Warren Buffett captures the essence of trust with his observation, "Trust is like the air we breathe—when it's present, nobody really notices; when it's absent, everybody notices."

Trust is the bedrock of professional reputation and credibility, serving not only as a mechanism for team cohesion but as a critical component in determining an individual's success and failure within an organization.

Being a trustworthy individual in a professional environment isn't just good for morale; it directly benefits you.

When you're seen as transparent, integrous, and dependable, you're not only making your workspace better, but you're also setting yourself up as a reliable and effective professional.

In this light, trustworthiness becomes the currency through which professional value is measured and acknowledged, paving the way for enhanced responsibilities, leadership opportunities, and, ultimately, career advancement.

No matter where you're at in your career, thinking you can go it alone is a mistake. The truth is, building strong relationships, fostering trust, and working effectively with others are what truly propel you forward. These aren't just nice-to-have qualities; they're must-haves.

So, if you're focusing solely on only being the best you can be technically in the hopes of advancing, you might want to pivot. Concentrate on being a team player and someone your colleagues can rely on. *That's* the stuff that takes you to the next level.

Let's look at the experiences of Charlie and Sam, both professionals with some years of experience under their belts. They approach work and career progression in two very different ways.

Charlie tackles the professional world with a laser focus on individual achievement. He is determined to be the *best* in everything he does. Everyday tasks are approached with a competitive edge, aiming to outshine others through superior performance and knowledge.

Charlie's intense focus on individual excellence and recognition leads him to guard his knowledge and expertise, treating information as a competitive advantage rather than a shared resource. He frequently works in isolation, preferring to solve problems alone to ensure credit goes solely to him.

This approach makes his colleagues reluctant to want to team with him, and equally hesitant to share their own insights, for fear that their contributions might either be overshadowed or appropriated. Consequently, this lack of openness and collaboration not only hampers the team's cooperative spirit but also fosters an environment of mistrust and rivalry.

As Charlie continues to prioritize his personal achievements over collective goals, the team dynamic suffers, with colleagues feeling compelled to safeguard their work and keep strategies to themselves to avoid being outperformed or marginalized.

In contrast, Sam realized long ago that trust and teamwork are undervalued currencies in the workplace. Rather than viewing colleagues as competitors, Sam sees them as partners in success. By taking the initiative to share insights, assist on projects simply to be helpful, and offer positive encouragement, Sam starts to weave a fabric of mutual support and collaboration within the team.

Over time, Sam's approach positively impacts the workplace culture. Each act of encouragement and teaming builds a foundation of trust not just in Sam's competence, but in their character. Colleagues know that when they turn to Sam for help, they receive not just assistance, but genuine investment in their success. This trust becomes reciprocal. Team members are more inclined to share their expertise, troubleshoot problems together, and approach projects with a collective spirit of innovation and openness.

This ethos of trustworthiness that Sam cultivates does more than just enhance the team's performance. It transforms the workplace into an environment where people feel valued, understood, and confident in their colleagues' support. This shift doesn't go unnoticed. This positive environment not only leads to higher job satisfaction but also positions Sam favorably for potential promotions and higher-level opportunities within the organization.

Charlie begins to notice the stark difference in how colleagues engage with Sam compared to the interactions they have with Charlie. Witnessing the genuine respect and camaraderie surrounding Sam, Charlie starts to reflect on the competitive walls built around them. It becomes apparent that the route to true professional success lies not in overshadowing others, but in uplifting them.

These narratives of Charlie and Sam illustrate a powerful lesson in professional growth—it's not merely about being the most knowledgeable or skilled individual. True career advancement, the kind that is both fulfilling and sustainable, is rooted in fostering trust and collaboration. Yes, technical competence is important, but trustworthiness and mutual respect among colleagues is just as, if not more, important to thrive in a career.

Trust as a Skill Set

Practically no one denies that trust and trustworthiness are essential aspects of business and work relationships, influencing every facet of our professional lives. Yet, very few discussions revolve around *how* to cultivate these qualities.

Often, trust is perceived as an innate attribute—you either have it or you don't. But what if you approached trust differently? What if you viewed it as a skill to be developed or a muscle to exercise and strengthen?

Much like any other critical skill in the workplace, from communication to technical expertise, trustworthiness can, and indeed should, be nurtured. Developing trust is about consistently demonstrating reliability, integrity, and sincerity in your interactions.

. . . .

WHAT IF YOU VIEWED TRUST AS A SKILL TO BE DEVELOPED OR A MUSCLE TO EXERCISE AND STRENGTHEN?

. . . .

It's about making commitments you can keep and always following through on your promises. Every completed task on time, every deadline met, and every honest conversation contributes to this narrative of reliability.

Moreover, trust as a skill means actively listening and showing empathy toward colleagues. It's about being transparent with your intentions and decisions, ensuring others understand your actions and motivations. Such openness not only humanizes you but also makes your actions predictable in a positive way, reinforcing others' belief in your trustworthiness.

Building trust also involves accepting accountability for your actions, particularly when things don't go as planned. Owning up to mistakes and learning from them demonstrates a level of integrity that others respect and trust.

Incorporating feedback is another facet of developing the trust muscle. Being open to critique, applying it constructively, and showing visible improvement or change based on that feedback, signals that you value others' perspectives and are committed to mutual success.

Like any skill, developing trust requires regular practice and conscious effort. It's about making small, consistent choices that, over time, culminate to establish a strong foundation of trustworthiness. By treating trust as a skill to be honed, you take control of your professional reputation and set the stage for deeper, more meaningful work interactions, time and time again.

Trust isn't a byproduct of success; as Richard Fagerlin observed, "Trust isn't what we do; it is what results from what we do." Building trust requires intention and effort. It starts with small commitments, like meeting deadlines consistently, openly sharing credit for success, or respecting confidences. Over time, these actions lay a foundation of reliability and integrity.

. . . .

BUILDING TRUST REQUIRES INTENTION AND EFFORT.

. . . .

What's Ahead?

We're excited for you to embark on a transformative journey through the pages of this book, designed exclusively for individuals keen on becoming indispensable in their professional spheres by mastering one critical skill: building trust. This guide is tailored to provide you with actionable insights and strategies to foster trust in every professional interaction, making you the go-to person in your workplace. Here's a glimpse of what we'll cover:

Why Is Trust Important?

Discover why trust transcends mere performance, learn about the profound benefits it brings to your career, and explore 12 reasons that underscore its significance. You'll understand how trust can elevate your standing and effectiveness at work, positioning you as a reliable and respected go-to person within your organization.

Should Trust Be Earned or Given?

Answer the age-old question of whether trust should be earned or given by delving into the subtleties of forming trust relationships, understanding the dynamic mechanics behind trust, and exploring its physiological roots. This chapter emphasizes the vital importance of reciprocity in the development of trust and advocates for a proactive approach to trusting, showcasing how it can lead to more open, effective, and enriching professional relationships.

Are You Trustworthy?

Featuring six elements of trust, this chapter provides a mirror for self-reflection. Apply these elements in your daily actions to significantly enhance your trustworthiness. By incorporating these traits, you solidify your reputation as dependable and competent.

Are You Inadvertently Eroding Trust?

Identify and rectify common, often overlooked behaviors that can undermine trust. Recognizing these pitfalls is the first step toward preventing unintentional harm to your relationships, ensuring the trust you've built remains intact and strong.

How Do You Trust When Out of Sight?

With remote work becoming increasingly common, this chapter tackles the challenges of building and maintaining trust in virtual settings. Fifteen actionable tips guide you through overcoming these hurdles, ensuring your team's cohesion and personal reliability flourish, irrespective of physical proximity.

How Do You Assess the Impact of Mistakes?

Mistakes are inevitable, but how they impact trust varies widely. The 'Trust Impact Matrix' serves as a tool to evaluate mistakes, like missing a deadline, understand their repercussions on trust, and guide you through more mindful navigation of errors and their fallout in the workplace.

How Do You Restore Trust After It Crumbles?

Learn effective strategies for mending trust, whether you're the aggrieved party or the one at fault. From apologies to actions, this chapter outlines the steps necessary to heal and rebuild trust, emphasizing the importance of accountability, transparency, and sincerity in repairing professional relationships.

Are You Nurturing or Neglecting Trust with Your Clients?

Learn practical strategies to build and maintain trust in client relationships, as well as recognize and address early signs of distrust. By understanding the actions that either foster or erode trust, you'll be equipped to strengthen client partnerships and turn potential weaknesses into growth opportunities.

How Do You Foster Trust Below and Above?

This chapter unveils the secrets to mastering trust in all directions—both upwards and downwards—redefining your influence in the workplace. Prepare to uncover practical strategies and techniques that will transform your leadership and team dynamics, building unshakable trust and positioning you as a pivotal force within your organization.

By focusing on trust within a professional setting, this book offers invaluable advice tailored specifically for individuals aiming to enhance their professional relationships. Through practical insights and actionable strategies, you will learn how to cultivate a reputation that exudes reliability, integrity, and competence—cornerstones of becoming the indispensable, go-to professional in any workplace.

TRUST QUESTION

· · · · · · · · · · · · · · · · ·

Who on your team embodies trust? How do their actions inspire others around them to become more trustful?

In every team, there are individuals whose presence and actions become the cornerstone of trust, shaping the culture and dynamics of the workspace. These individuals aren't just participants in trust; they are its creators, fostering an environment where open communication, reliability, and integrity flourish. Here are a few actions that personify trust and inspire trust around them:

1. **Consistent Transparency:** They communicate openly, sharing both the good news and the challenges. This transparency doesn't just keep everyone informed; it invites a shared sense of responsibility and unity.

2. **Reliability in Action:** When they commit, they deliver. This reliability builds a scaffold of dependability that others feel confident leaning on, knowing promises will be kept and expectations met.

3. **Empathetic Listening:** They show genuine interest in the concerns and ideas of their colleagues. By actively listening and validating others' perspectives, they cultivate an environment where everyone feels heard and valued.

4. **Acknowledging and Celebrating Successes:** Recognizing the contributions and achievements of others, no matter how small, reinforces the importance of every individual's role and nurtures a culture of appreciation and respect.

Trust is not just about having confidence in someone's abilities; it's about building a foundation where mutual respect, open communication, and shared goals lead to a thriving and collaborative workspace.

WHY IS TRUST IMPORTANT?

▶ The Myth That Performance Trumps All

In today's fast-paced workforce, performance typically takes center stage. A quick glimpse at any modern workplace reveals a universe where metrics, objectives, and achievements rule supreme.

We live in an era of quantifiable success, where feedback and compensation systems meticulously measure every output, every accomplishment, and every key stroke. Indeed, performance is pivotal. It's the heartbeat of business growth and the scaffold of career advancement.

But here's the catch—in the fervent quest to top performance charts, the elemental human factor of trust can be frequently left by the wayside.

So, let's talk about trust. Not the "cross my heart" kind, but the robust, foundational trust that transforms work into a highly motivational and rewarding experience. This trust is the catalyst that elevates work from mere transactions of time and skill into meaningful collaborations that generate innovation, respect, and unparalleled success. It's the kind of trust that turns routines into rituals, tasks into passions, and individuals into fiercely united teams.

However, in a landscape captivated by performance metrics, trust doesn't quite fit the mold. You can't neatly package it into PowerPoint slides or Excel sheets. Trust doesn't scream for attention in the monthly review meetings, nor does it easily translate into quantifiable data on annual reports.

Its presence, or lack thereof, is felt rather than quantified. Yet, paradoxically, trust is what elevates good contributors to great performers, transforming groups of individuals into coherent, unstoppable teams.

So, why is trust often sidelined?

Partly because it's harder to build and maintain than writing the perfect report or hitting your targeted goals. Trust demands consistency, empathy, transparency, and, most crucially, time—elements that are often in short supply in high-pressure work environments. And yet, it's this very trust that could be the linchpin for unparalleled performance and satisfaction.

To become an indispensable and go-to team member, start by cultivating behaviors that unequivocally establish your trustworthiness. Being seen as extremely trustworthy doesn't just happen overnight; it's built through consistent and deliberate actions.

Reflect on how your own actions can either build or erode trust. Are you actively demonstrating competence by delivering tasks with excellence and continually striving for improvement? Do your actions reflect a commitment to openness, characterized by sharing information willingly and engaging transparently? By consistently applying your skills, sharing insights, and upholding a standard of excellence, you affirm your reliability and contribute to a foundation of trust.

BEING SEEN AS EXTREMELY TRUSTWORTHY DOESN'T JUST HAPPEN OVERNIGHT; IT'S BUILT THROUGH CONSISTENT AND DELIBERATE ACTIONS.

Do you recognize and celebrate the achievements of your colleagues, thereby fostering an environment of empowerment? Acknowledging the hard work and success of team members not only affirms their value but also enhances your role as a supportive and trusted ally.

How often do you engage in dialogue that demonstrates genuine interest and understanding of your teammates' views and experiences? Promoting open communication and actively practicing empathy by considering and understanding team members' perspectives and feelings further nurtures a culture of trust.

Prioritizing these behaviors to enhance trust can transform your professional relationships and elevate your standing within any team. By embodying trustworthiness in every interaction, you not only become a model team member but also an active contributor in the quest for collective success. In the end, your reputation as a trustworthy individual will precede you, making you the go-to person in any project or team.

All for One or One for All?

Trust in the workplace profoundly influences every individual's experience, shaping how they engage in daily tasks and interact with colleagues. Whether sharing ideas or managing responsibilities, the level of trust you perceive and develop in your environment can either enrich your professional growth or hinder your progress amidst ongoing conflicts. Let's explore relationships without trust and those with trust to gain a clearer understanding of its impact.

Relationships Without Trust

The weight of skepticism can heavily burden the atmosphere of a workplace. Distrust between colleagues manifests in a myriad of ways, often leading to toxic and inefficient work relationships and environments. This environment might make you overly cautious and insecure, afraid to make mistakes or share important thoughts.

As suspicion escalates, communication breaks down, leading to increased misunderstandings and conflict. This not only stifles innovation but also creates an environment where negativity thrives, further impeding productivity and collaboration.

Here are firsthand accounts that vividly illustrate the real-world consequences of a lack of trust between teammates:

- "I find myself double-checking my work obsessively before submitting it, because one small error will result in a flood of blame rather than constructive criticism."

- "When there's a deadline, the pressure is overwhelming because I don't trust my teammates to deliver their parts, which means I often end up feeling like I have to do it all."

- "Every time my phone rings with a call from this one colleague, I immediately feel anxious, wondering what I did wrong now, since past interactions have always been so critical."

- "I keep my suggestions to myself in meetings because I've seen others get shot down or ridiculed when they propose something new. I don't trust my team to be any different with me."

- "Even when I'm sick, I hesitate to call out because I don't trust that my colleagues will cover for me, or worse, they'll resent me for leaving them with extra work."

- "In meetings, I often remain silent, even if I think something is off, because I don't trust that my colleagues won't dismiss or belittle my concerns."

- "I never volunteer for joint projects if I can help it; the lack of trust between us means pulling more than my own weight to meet the objectives."

- "I find myself keeping useful information close to the chest, as I don't trust my coworkers to give credit where it's due if they use it."

- "When there's conflict within the team, I just keep out of it because I don't trust us to come together and resolve it without holding grudges."

- "I avoid giving genuine compliments to my colleagues as the competitive environment has eroded my trust. I fear they might see it as just being manipulative or disingenuous."

The scenarios described highlight the troubling outcomes when trust is lacking between colleagues. A work environment without trust becomes filled with tension, suspicion, and hesitancy, impeding both cooperation and individual performance. In stark contrast, the presence of trust can lead to a more effective and supportive partnership, where colleagues work confidently and constructively, knowing they can rely on one another.

Relationships With Trust

When you feel secure in the trust you share with colleagues, communication becomes effortless, and managing your work is more efficient and effective. This atmosphere of trust creates a nurturing environment that facilitates your own growth and personal excellence.

Here, cooperation comes naturally, and challenges are tackled with a shared resilience. Mistakes become opportunities for personal growth rather than occasions for criticism, creating an atmosphere where you feel appreciated, understood, and supported.

. . . .

WHEN YOU FEEL SECURE IN THE TRUST YOU SHARE WITH COLLEAGUES, COMMUNICATION BECOMES EFFORTLESS, AND MANAGING YOUR WORK IS MORE EFFICIENT AND EFFECTIVE.

. . . .

In such an environment, not only do daily operations run smoothly, but there's also a quick and efficient adaptation to change and uncertainty, supported by a collective resoluteness and shared vision. Trust serves as the foundation of your creative contributions, where your ideas are encouraged and valued rather than dismissed.

The following testimonials shine a light on the profound difference that trust can make, painting a picture of the positive dynamics that flourish in its presence:

- "When I make a mistake, I don't fear telling my team because I know we trust each other to understand and work together on a solution, rather than point fingers."

- "I trust my colleague so much that when she gives me feedback, I know it's for my growth and not out of spite; this openness has really helped me excel."

- "Managing projects is a breeze because my team trusts me to delegate tasks. They know that I've got their backs if any issues arise."

- "I can share my unique ideas in team meetings with confidence, trusting that my peers will listen and consider them thoughtfully, even if they challenge the status quo."

- "If I need to leave work early for a personal commitment, I trust that my colleagues understand and support my work-life balance, as I would do the same for them."

- "During brainstorming sessions, I can freely bounce my wildest ideas off my coworkers, trusting that they'll engage with them seriously and help refine them."

- "When feedback is given, I take it as a gift because I trust that my colleague is looking out for my best interests, aiming to help me improve rather than merely criticize."

- "I didn't hesitate to ask for help when I was overwhelmed. I knew I could trust my colleague not to view it as a weakness, but as a normal part of teamwork."

- "Knowing that I can trust my colleagues to respect confidentiality, I am open in sharing information that helps us all do our jobs better without fearing information leakage."

- "I feel comfortable going on vacation knowing that my projects are in good hands with my colleagues, trusting they will handle things just as I would."

The stark contrast between an environment lacking trust and one abundant with it underscores the transformative impact of trust on your work experience. Without trust, your job can become a lone battle for survival, but with a solid foundation of trust, the same workplace becomes a source of flourishing collaboration and support.

Embracing and fostering trust is crucial, not merely for enhancing your productivity but also for carving out a space where you can thrive and feel fulfilled. This dedication to cultivating and upholding trust is not just advantageous—it is vital for your growth and for the enduring success of any organization you're part of.

12 Reasons Why You Should Care About Trust

Let's face it—no one prefers a workplace simmering with suspicion over one blooming with trust. Yet, acknowledging trust's value and actively cultivating it can require effort, patience, and time.

Why should you prioritize building trust above other important tasks and time commitments?

Here are 12 thought-provoking, compelling reasons that showcase why embedding trust in your work DNA isn't just a 'nice-to-have', but a game-changing strategy everyone should care deeply about:

Facilitates Open Communication: When trust is present, you feel comfortable openly sharing your thoughts, feedback, and concerns, leading to clearer and more productive conversations.

Enhances Collaboration: Trust makes it easier for you to work side by side with your colleagues, sharing responsibilities effortlessly, and collaboratively tackling projects.

Empowers Decision-Making: Trust diminishes your fears, empowering you to make decisions confidently and without undue worry about failure.

Increases Productivity: With trusting relationships, you experience less stress and fewer distractions, which enables you to focus better on your tasks and increase your productivity.

Improves Morale: Trust contributes to a positive atmosphere at your workplace, boosting your job satisfaction and overall work experience.

Supports Innovation: In a trusting environment, you feel more secure sharing innovative ideas and taking calculated risks, paving the way for creative solutions and advancements.

Encourages Professional Growth: Trust encourages you to seek and offer constructive feedback, engage in mentorship, and provide support, all of which propel your personal and professional development.

Reduces Conflicts: Trust helps you avoid misunderstandings and conflicts preemptively; and when disagreements do arise, they are resolved easily.

Strengthens Loyalty: Trust fosters strong bonds with team members, enhancing mutual loyalty which contributes to higher retention and a stronger commitment to the organization.

Promotes Autonomy: With trust, you feel confident in your colleagues' capabilities, which empowers you to ask for help without feeling the need for constant oversight, promoting a sense of independence.

Builds a Supportive Environment: A trusting relationship means you and your colleagues are more likely to support each other during challenging times, ensuring no one feels overwhelmed or isolated.

Encourages Honesty: In a trusting environment, you feel safe to share your opinion or perspective without fear of repercussion.

Considering these 12 strong reasons, let's visualize the workplace as if it were a well-maintained garden. In this setting, trust is essential, like water, ensuring everything grows healthily and effectively without any stagnation.

Trust as Water: Trust acts like a crucial nutrient, ensuring you feel appreciated and connected. It keeps the work environment healthy and prevents it from becoming unproductive.

Open Communication as Sunlight: Open discussions encourage transparency and the emergence of new ideas, similar to how sunlight supports plant growth. This openness leads to achieving collective goals.

Collaboration as Soil: Working together combines different strengths and abilities, just like soil provides the necessary nutrients for plants. This teamwork lays the groundwork for success.

Productivity as Flowers: Achievements in work are like flowers blooming, showing the results of your hard work and contributing to a positive and successful atmosphere.

Morale as Bees: High spirits keep the workplace lively, spreading positivity like bees pollinate flowers, reminding everyone of the importance of staying motivated and connected.

Innovation as Fruit: Taking risks and innovating can lead to unexpected and rewarding outcomes, representing the fruits of your labor that showcase the team's ability to push boundaries and succeed.

Professional Growth as Pruning: Removing what's unnecessary and focusing on what contributes to growth is crucial. This trimming process helps improve skills and career paths.

Conflicts as Weeds: Addressing disagreements promptly prevents them from undermining the team's progress, maintaining harmony and productivity just as removing weeds protects a garden's health.

Loyalty as Perennials: Deep commitment and dedication are vital, providing a stable and enduring presence in the team, much like perennials anchor a garden throughout the seasons.

Autonomy as Space: Having the freedom to explore and contribute uniquely is essential. Autonomy encourages diversity and personal growth, akin to plants needing space to flourish.

Decision-Making as Rain: Making empowered decisions helps overcome setbacks and fosters exploration in different directions, similar to how rain supports plants in growing stronger.

Honesty as Compost: Being honest turns challenges into opportunities for improvement and strengthens relationships, enriching the team's resolve and collaboration, much like compost nourishes a garden.

This garden metaphor transforms the abstract concept of a workplace into a living ecosystem, illustrating how crucial each element is to the collective health and success. Just as a garden's beauty stems from its diversity and mutual dependencies, so too does the strength of a workplace emerge from its collaborative spirit, nurtured by trust and tended with care.

The Necessity of Vulnerability

In professional settings, building trust among colleagues and within teams goes beyond simply aligning on objectives or cooperatively tackling projects; it hinges on the personal relationships that underpin a successful work atmosphere.

Vulnerability, often misconceived as a weakness, proves to be vital for robust work relationships, promoting stronger bonds and fostering genuine trust. Balancing this openness with clear personal and professional boundaries cultivates a respectful and coherent team dynamic.

. . . .

**VULNERABILITY, OFTEN MISCONCEIVED
AS A WEAKNESS, PROVES TO BE VITAL
FOR ROBUST WORK RELATIONSHIPS.**

. . . .

Vulnerability as a Strength

Vulnerability in the workplace was once largely regarded as taboo—a liability that could expose one to judgment or criticism. Yet, this perception is changing. Showing vulnerability is increasingly seen as a cornerstone of leadership and a catalyst for strong teamwork. When you openly share your challenges, uncertainties, or lack of answers, it does not reflect incompetence. Instead, it showcases your humanness, bravery, and willingness to seek collaboration.

This authentic self-representation acts as an invitation for others to engage in similar openness, promoting a culture where ideas and innovations are shared without fear of failure or ridicule. It dismantles the façade of infallibility that you may feel pressured to maintain, paving the way for a more genuine expression of concerns, aspirations, and limitations. Such an atmosphere not only invites diverse perspectives but also empowers you and others to contribute their best, knowing that vulnerability will not be exploited, but rather supported.

In practical terms, vulnerability can translate into transparent discussions about your workload, admitting when you don't have the answer, or requesting help when you're stuck. It can also mean sharing personal anecdotes that illuminate your values or what you find challenging. This level of openness fosters a sense of shared humanity, laying a robust groundwork for trust. Colleagues who see vulnerability expressed with integrity tend to reciprocate in kind, fostering an environment where trust is not merely a concept but a lived experience.

Setting Boundaries While Being Open

Handling vulnerability responsibly, however, also means recognizing the importance of establishing boundaries.

Being open does not entail oversharing or operating without filters; rather, it is about discerning what to share, with whom, and under what circumstances. Boundaries are the safeguards that prevent vulnerability from tipping into overexposure, ensuring that openness serves its purpose: to build trust, not to erode it.

Setting boundaries requires a clear understanding of your comfort levels, communication of expectations, and respect for others' limits. It means knowing when to say no, asking for time when needed, and protecting your own well-being and the well-being of the team. Boundaries give structure to vulnerability, shaping it into a powerful tool for connection rather than a source of unnecessary emotional strain.

In essence, vulnerability combined with clear boundaries can help create a team culture where individuals feel safe to be their authentic selves. It can serve as a force for good, promoting resilience and adaptability. When people know that their openness is appreciated but not exploited, and when they understand the importance of stewarding their personal boundaries, a symbiotic relationship between vulnerability and trust can flourish.

As paradoxical as it may seem, embracing vulnerability is an act of professional strength. When handled with care and coupled with the discipline of boundary-setting, it forms the bedrock of trust in any working relationship. By allowing yourself to be seen—your strengths, your weaknesses, your successes, and your struggles—you pave the way for truly resilient and collaborative workplace culture, where trust is not just an outcome, but a practice integrated into every interaction.

What's In It for You to Trust

Embracing trust within your workplace can dramatically transform your professional and personal life for the better, a fact underscored by insights from "Being with Trust" by Harvard Business Review. Here's what cultivating a high-trust environment could mean for you:

- Imagine waking up to significantly less stress—about 74% less, to be precise. The weight of worry and apprehension that often accompanies an average workday diminishes when you're part of a high-trust organization. This reduction in stress is not just a number; it's a palpable change that could redefine your workday and contribute to a healthier, happier life.

- With trust as the foundation of your workplace, you'll likely find yourself invigorated with over 100% more energy at work. This isn't just about having the stamina to tackle your to-do list; it's about bringing an enthusiastic mindset to your projects, igniting creativity, and inspiring those around you.

- Productivity sees a notable leap—50% higher—in environments rich in trust. Tasks that seemed daunting before become manageable because you're empowered to approach them in ways that best suit your skills and creativity, without the constant weight of micromanagement or skepticism.

- Engagement with your work and your colleagues soars by 76% in a high trust setting. Engagement means more than just showing up; it means being mentally and emotionally invested in your job, leading to richer collaborations and more satisfying outcomes.

- The benefits also extend beyond the office. Experiencing 29% more satisfaction with life overall, trust helps you find a more fulfilling balance between your professional and personal worlds. The positivity that emanates from trusting work relationships spills over into other areas of your life, enriching your overall well-being.

- Lastly, consider the impact on burnout—an issue many face in today's challenging work environments.

In a high-trust organization, the incidence of burnout drops by 40%. Trust acts as a buffer against the pressures that cause fatigue and disillusionment, letting you find more joy and motivation in your efforts.

In adopting a mindset that prioritizes trust, you're not just enhancing your professional life; you're taking a significant step toward more profound contentment and resilience in all facets of your existence. The science speaks volumes: Building and nurturing trust is one of the most potent moves you can make for a richer, more rewarding life, both within and outside the workplace.

BUILDING AND NURTURING TRUST IS ONE OF THE MOST POTENT MOVES YOU CAN MAKE FOR A RICHER, MORE REWARDING LIFE.

TRUST QUESTION

· · · · · · · · · · · · · · · · · ·

**How does it feel when a colleague places
their trust in you? Does it incentivize you
to behave in any particular way in return?**

Trust is no less than the heartbeat of professional relationships. It's an invisible thread that binds teams and drives performance. When trust is reciprocated, it's transformative. But what about at the individual level, between colleagues? Here are some common scenarios:

Delegating Crucial Tasks: When a colleague delegates or asks you for help on an important task, it's a vote of confidence in your abilities. This trust often drives you to live up to their expectations, leading you to do your best job possible.

Sharing Sensitive Information: Receiving sensitive or confidential information from a peer is testimony to their trust in your discretion. The responsibility assumes respectfulness in dealing with such information, strengthening the bond of trust, and underscores your own integrity.

Backing in a Dispute: When a colleague backs you in a disagreement, it shows they trust your judgment. This kind of trust can evoke a lifetime of loyalty and mutual respect toward that colleague.

Seeking Advice: If a colleague comes to you for advice, it tells you they trust your expertise and value your opinion. This encourages you to reciprocate that vulnerability, fostering a culture of shared growth.

When trust is extended by a colleague, recognizing this gesture becomes crucial. This act of faith merits thoughtful reciprocation, which can significantly strengthen professional bonds. Every gesture of trust offers an opportunity not just to appreciate the confidence placed in you but also to demonstrate your reliability and commitment in return, thereby reinforcing a cycle of trust that is beneficial for all involved.

SHOULD TRUST BE EARNED OR GIVEN?

Imagine walking into your new office—a space teeming with potential allies, adversaries, and acquaintances. Do you bestow your confidence upon your coworkers from day one, or do you require them to prove their reliability through their actions? Amid the myriad interactions and transactions of your professional life, the stance you adopt on this issue could define the very tenor of your career.

What has been your approach so far? Do you find yourself instinctively extending trust, or are you more guarded, cautiously appraising each colleague's trustworthiness over time? Reflect on the relationships you have formed—which ones flourished, and which withered on the vine? Consider how your initial choice to grant or withhold trust may have set the stage for these outcomes.

As you ponder these questions, think also about how you perceive and project trustworthiness. Are you conscious of the signals you send to your colleagues? Are your actions consistently aligned with your words? And, when others entrust you with their confidence, do you acknowledge and reciprocate it? The interplay of giving and earning trust is not just a one-way street; it involves a continual, dynamic exchange between all parties.

Do you recall a moment when someone's gesture of trust caught you by surprise and perhaps even inspired you to be more open in turn? Contrast that with a time when you felt someone's trust had to be patiently earned, thread by painstaking thread. What were the outcomes of these different approaches? Did one method foster a stronger bond, or were they merely different paths to the same destination?

Remember, no work environment is immune to the trials and tribulations of trust. The decision to extend or withhold trust is one you will make time and again. It is not merely a philosophical stance but a practical strategy that, when thoughtfully employed, can profoundly influence the dynamics of your workplace.

As we delve into the upcoming narratives of Anna and Ben, consider their story through the lens of your experiences. How do the notions of the dynamics of trust, the physiological effects of the hormone oxytocin, and the vital aspect of reciprocity resonate with you? Have you witnessed the unfolding of these elements in your interactions? How might understanding these concepts help you navigate the delicate landscape of workplace relationships?

We invite you to join us in unpacking these layers, exploring examples from the work life of our two characters, and examining their implications in your professional sphere. Should trust be earned, or should it be given? As you turn these pages and walk the corridors of your own workplace, what will your answer be?

Unveiling the Dynamics of Trust

In the bustling world of modern workplaces, trust forms the cornerstone of effective and harmonious collaborations. Let's consider colleagues Anna and Ben, navigating the complexities of teamwork while pursuing shared goals. Trust, for them, begins with small yet significant gestures.

Anna, for instance, decides to take the first step in building this bridge of trust by being completely transparent about her decision-making processes with Ben. She doesn't shy away from admitting her uncertainties about certain project decisions, allows Ben to take the lead on segments where he has more expertise, openly acknowledges any mistakes she makes, and shares personal insights that shed light on her working style and ethics.

These actions, though seemingly simple, are Anna's way of saying, "I trust you, Ben." This is trust as an action, a voluntary vulnerability she chooses to display, signaling to Ben her willingness to open up and depend on him.

The Oxytocin Connection

Ben's response to Anna's openness is not just emotional or cognitive; it's physiological. The human brain, wired to respond to signals of trust, initiates a release of oxytocin—often referred to as the "bonding hormone"—in response to these trust signals. This hormone plays a pivotal role in social connection, influencing feelings of attachment and connection.

When Ben witnesses Anna's acts of trust toward him, his brain's oxytocin levels spike, enhancing his sense of connection to Anna and, crucially, motivating him to reciprocate the trust she has shown. It's a biological incentive to strengthen the bond, fostering a mutual sense of trustworthiness and dependency.

Reciprocity: The Lifeblood of Trust

Driven by an increased level of oxytocin, Ben finds himself more inclined to engage in acts of trust toward Anna. This could manifest in various ways: perhaps he shares critical feedback with her, knowing that it will be received constructively, or he might confide in her about his concerns and aspirations regarding the project they're working on.

This exchange of trust and vulnerability, facilitated by their rising oxytocin levels, fosters a deeper connection and understanding between the two. It transforms their interaction from mere cooperation to a partnership characterized by mutual respect and reliance.

However, trust is not without its perils. Initially, when Anna chose to be open and vulnerable with Ben, she did so without the assurance of reciprocity. This vulnerability is the crux of trust—it is inherently risky. Without risk, trust cannot bloom, nor can it invoke the biological rewards that sustain it.

Moreover, for trust to thrive and grow, it must be reciprocal. If Anna were the only one extending trust without Ben engaging in kind, the imbalance could prompt her to retract, potentially stymieing the development of their relationship.

. . . .

FOR TRUST TO THRIVE AND GROW, IT MUST BE RECIPROCAL.

. . . .

This reciprocity is essential; it's what ensures that both parties remain engaged in this delicate dance of trust. As both Anna and Ben continue to reciprocate trust, they not only reinforce their bond but also pave the way for a more dynamic and coherent teamwork experience.

In essence, for Anna and Ben—just as for anyone navigating the complex dynamics of workplace relationships—trust involves an ongoing, reciprocal exchange of vulnerability and support. It's marked by the willingness to take risks and the physiological underpinnings that make such interpersonal investments worthwhile. Through mutual trust, Anna and Ben transcend mere co-worker status, fostering a collaborative spirit that enhances their productivity and enriches their professional journey together.

As we conclude this exploration of trust within the workplace, encapsulated through the experiences of Anna and Ben, it's clear that trust serves as the foundation of robust professional relationships. Their stories offer valuable insights, but more critically, they push us toward a compelling proposition: the proactive giving of trust as a default stance in professional interactions.

Giving trust freely, as opposed to waiting for it to be earned, can transform the dynamics of workplace relationships. It creates an environment of openness and mutual respect, where collaboration flourishes and innovation thrive. This approach, exemplified by Anna's early openness with her colleague, facilitates a quicker breakdown of barriers and speeds up the process of teaming.

GIVING TRUST FREELY, AS OPPOSED TO WAITING FOR IT TO BE EARNED, CAN TRANSFORM THE DYNAMICS OF WORKPLACE RELATIONSHIPS.

Consider your own workplace. Imagine the potential changes in atmosphere and productivity if trust were not a commodity to be earned with effort and time, but a gift given at the onset of every professional interaction. This is not to suggest a reckless abandonment of discretion, but rather an encouragement to lean into trust, to err on the side of openness.

Reflect on the reciprocal nature of trust. When you initiate this cycle by extending trust, you are not only setting a positive tone but also inviting others to respond in kind. This mutual exchange not only fosters a supportive working environment but also enhances everyone's capacity to be vulnerable and innovative without fear of undue judgment or reprisal.

Being trustworthy, then, becomes an act of responsibility and integrity. It means consistently aligning actions with promises, acknowledging mistakes, and respecting the trust placed in you by others. It becomes less about safeguarding oneself from potential breaches of trust, and more about contributing to a culture where trust circulates freely and enriches all interactions.

As you step back into the flow of your daily professional life, armed with these insights, consider the transformative possibility of choosing to give trust freely. What opportunities might open up? How might relationships deepen? How might team dynamics improve?

The decision to give trust freely should not be viewed merely as a risk, but as a personal commitment to fostering a culture of openness and integrity. This approach not only showcases your integrity but also sets a standard for personal interactions within the workplace. It creates a positive feedback loop of trustworthiness and respect, enhancing not just your own relationships but also inspiring others to emulate this trusting behavior.

This voluntary extension of trust can thereby transform the interpersonal dynamics around you, encouraging a more supportive and understanding work environment. Therefore, let this be more than just a theoretical exercise. ***Consider it a call to action.***

Choose to be the initiator of trust in your workplace. Set forth a new paradigm where trust is the opening rather than the conclusion and observe how this shift can remarkably alter the landscape of your professional relationships, shaping a more collaborative, innovative, and trusting environment.

TRUST QUESTION

· · · · · · · · · · · · · · · · ·

When has taking a risk in trusting a colleague led to a positive outcome? What did you learn from it?

There was a particular moment in my career that under-lined the true value of trust among peers. I had been work-ing tirelessly on a project proposal due to be presented to our senior management. It was a proposal I believed could significantly impact our team's direction and success. But, as deadlines approached, I found myself overwhelmed with the sheer volume of work still needed to polish it to perfection.

At this critical juncture, I made a decision to trust a peer with whom I'd shared many brainstorming sessions but never officially collaborated on a project. Despite having a similar workload, this colleague had always shown a pro-found understanding of our project's vision and objectives.

I took a leap of faith and asked for their help in refining and finalizing the proposal. This move was a risk; it involved handing over parts of a project I'd closely nurtured, with the hope that they would not only understand my perspective but enhance it with their insights.

The results were nothing short of remarkable. Not only did my colleague deliver, but they also added layers of depth and analysis I hadn't fully explored. Their contri-butions were instrumental in us receiving an enthusiastic green light from senior management, an accomplishment that significantly benefited our team and highlighted the innovative capacity we could achieve through collaboration. Here's what this experience taught me:

- **There is Strength in Diversity:** Trusting my colleague brought a new and diverse perspective to the project, something I couldn't have achieved working in isolation. This diversity of thought is critical in creating comprehensive solutions.

- **Shared Success Is More Fulfilling:** The success we achieved through our collaboration was incredibly rewarding. Sharing in this success created a sense of collective achievement and belonging within our team.

- **Trust Breaks Down Silos:** This experience was a powerful reminder that trust is a key enabler in breaking down silos. It fostered a more inclusive and collaborative team environment that encouraged others to seek help and offer assistance.

Trusting a peer, especially in high-stakes situations, might seem daunting, but it's a testament to the incredible outcomes teams can achieve when trust is placed at the heart of collaboration.

ARE YOU TRUSTWORTHY?

In the realm of workplace dynamics, establishing and nurturing trust is not just beneficial but essential. Trust acts as the backbone of effective working relationships, teams, and businesses, fostering environments where creativity, productivity, and mutual respect flourish. The essence of trust can be distilled into six pivotal elements: Competence, Openness, Integrity, Empathy, Empowerment, and Consistency. Each element plays a unique role in weaving a tapestry of reliance and confidence among colleagues.

Elements of Trust

Competence is often the first measure of trustworthiness that comes to mind in a professional setting. It involves more than just having a set of skills or a list of achievements; it's about embodying the capability to execute tasks with a level of excellence that inspires confidence.

Competence means staying ahead in one's area of expertise, continuously learning, and applying knowledge in ways that not only meet but exceed expectations. When a colleague demonstrates competence, they become a pillar of reliability within the team, someone who can be counted on to deliver when it matters most. This reliability not only empowers the individual but elevates the performance and trust within the team.

Openness in the workplace is akin to the windows in a house—it lets in the light and allows for a clear view inside. It's about being communicative, sharing necessary information without reservation, and embracing transparency. When individuals practice openness, it dismantles barriers between roles and hierarchies, encouraging everyone to share ideas and feedback.

Such a culture not only accelerates innovation but also fosters a deep sense of belonging and value among team members. When you know your insights are welcomed and your contributions acknowledged, the workplace transforms into a space of mutual respect and collaborative effort.

Integrity serves as the moral compass in professional relationships, guiding actions and decisions with a sense of responsibility and honesty. It's about aligning actions with values, ensuring promises are kept, and facing challenges with direct and fair solutions. This dedication to principle fosters a culture where reliability is not just expected but celebrated.

Integrity builds a foundation of dependability. Colleagues know they can count on each other to do the right thing, even when it's hard. Such a steadfast commitment to ethical behavior strengthens the team's resilience in the face of adversity. This element of trust is crucial in maintaining an ethical workplace where everyone feels respected and integral to the team.

Empathy goes beyond simple understanding; it's about genuinely connecting with teammates on a human level. By practicing empathy, individuals foster an environment where everyone feels seen and heard. This deep sense of connection ensures that team members are more engaged and motivated to contribute to collective goals.

It's about listening actively, acknowledging different perspectives, and valuing each person's unique contributions.

Empathy in the workplace leads to stronger, more cohesive teams that can navigate challenges with a sense of unity and compassion. Without empathy, problem-solving becomes a task rather than a shared mission, stripping the work of its human essence and creative potential.

Empowerment is about bestowing trust and autonomy to colleagues, demonstrating confidence in their capabilities and judgment. It's an uplifting force that motivates individuals to own their tasks, make decisions, and innovate within their roles.

Empowerment encourages a proactive attitude, where team members are driven not by directives but by a shared vision and trust in their abilities. When people feel empowered, they are more likely to take initiative and strive for excellence, knowing they have the support and trust of their colleagues and leaders.

Consistency is what binds all these elements together over time and transforms individual actions into a predictable pattern of behavior. Trust isn't built overnight nor maintained with sporadic effort. It requires a continuous, steadfast commitment to uphold these values day in and day out.

Consistency means applying competence, openness, integrity, empathy, and empowerment repeatedly, in every interaction and decision. It assures colleagues that the trustworthiness they see today will be the trustworthiness they experience tomorrow. This reliability becomes the foundation upon which all successful professional relationships are built.

Trust is far from a static or simple concept; it's a living, evolving connection between individuals. It's something that, once established, needs to be nurtured and maintained through ongoing effort and commitment. Integrating these six elements into the fabric of daily interactions transforms workplaces into arenas of mutual respect, innovation, and unshakeable trust.

TRUST IS FAR FROM A STATIC OR SIMPLE CONCEPT; IT'S A LIVING, EVOLVING CONNECTION BETWEEN INDIVIDUALS.

Elements in Action

Bridging the gap between the foundational elements of trust and their practical application in everyday scenarios is pivotal for realizing a truly collaborative and effective workplace. It is through the conscientious application of these principles, embodied in specific behaviors and practices, that the abstract qualities of trust are translated into concrete outcomes.

This shift from theory to practice is essential for cultivating an atmosphere of mutual respect, innovation, and unwavering trust. Here is what you can do to transition the theoretical aspects of trust into consistent, everyday actions.

Competence

- Take the time to thoroughly review your work for accuracy before submitting it to ensure that it reflects your high standards and attention to detail.

- Commit to your professional development by actively seeking out learning opportunities, and then generously share your new knowledge with your team to contribute to a culture of continuous improvement.

- Request constructive feedback on your work and genuinely consider the input, showing your openness to evolve and enhance the quality of your output.

- Bring forth unique and actionable ideas during team discussions, manifesting your innovative thinking and deep comprehension of what works in your industry.

- When errors occur, acknowledge your part without defensiveness and focus on finding solutions quickly, building trust through responsible and proactive behavior.

Openness

- Actively share updates about your work and progress in team meetings, making sure everyone is informed and on the same page, fostering a culture of transparency.

- Encourage your colleagues to voice their ideas and opinions, and genuinely listen to what they have to say, thereby creating an environment where diverse perspectives are valued.

- Openly discuss the challenges you're facing with your work in team discussions, seeking input and assistance, which can lead to innovative solutions and collaborative problem-solving.

- Proactively communicate any changes in project timelines or scope to all stakeholders involved, ensuring that expectations are realigned and misunderstandings are minimized.

- When making decisions, explain your reasoning to those affected, offering transparency into your thought process and building trust through clear communication.

Integrity

- Honor your commitments to your team by completing tasks you have agreed to take on, showing that your word holds value and can be trusted.

- Admit to and take responsibility for your mistakes rather than hiding them or placing blame elsewhere, demonstrating accountability and a commitment to learning and improvement.

- Protect confidential information shared by your teammates, showing that you are a trustworthy and dependable confidant for sensitive matters.

- Treat everyone with fairness and respect, regardless of their position or opinion, ensuring a workplace environment that values dignity and equality.

- Make decisions that align with both the organization's values and your own personal ethical standards, reinforcing a culture of integrity and ethical conduct.

Empathy

- Actively listen when your colleagues share their concerns or achievements, showing interest and understanding, and making them feel genuinely heard and supported.

- Offer your assistance to colleagues who are overwhelmed, showing that you recognize their hard work and are there to support them as a team member.

- Approach disagreements with a desire to understand the other person's perspective, which can lead to more productive and respectful resolutions.

- Celebrate your coworkers' personal milestones or acknowledge their personal situations, such as wishing them well before they take a parental leave or expressing condolences in difficult times.

- Encourage an inclusive atmosphere by inviting quieter team members to share their thoughts during meetings, ensuring that everyone has an opportunity to contribute.

Empowerment

- Ask your colleagues to help you with tasks, showing that you trust in their abilities to handle important responsibilities, thereby fostering their growth and independence.

- Encourage your team members to make decisions within their domain, demonstrating your confidence in their judgment and supporting them in taking ownership.

- Trust your colleagues to lead projects or meetings, giving them the platform to showcase their leadership and organizational skills, thereby instilling confidence in their abilities.

- Provide constructive feedback that focuses on strengths and potential for growth, rather than solely on areas of improvement, to boost their confidence and skill development.

- Offer resources and tools that enable your colleagues to innovate and improve their workflow, thereby supporting their autonomy and creative problem-solving efforts.

Consistency

- Ensure that you communicate regularly and transparently with your colleagues, keeping them informed about project statuses, changes, and your own availability.

- Attend and be punctual for scheduled meetings consistently. When you say you will be somewhere or do something at a specific time, follow through every time.

- Strive to produce work of high quality. Whether it's a routine task or a high-stakes project, apply the same level of care and detail to ensure that your colleagues can rely on your outputs.

- Respond to emails, messages, and requests in a timely manner regularly. Consistency in your response time shows that you are dependable.

- Offer your help frequently, not just during high-profile projects or when you have something to gain. Regular support fosters a dependable work environment.

Having explored the multifaceted nature of trust within the workplace, it becomes evident that each component—Competence, Openness, Integrity, Empathy, Empowerment, and Consistency—serves a critical role in cultivating an environment where trust thrives.

As we have broken down these elements, illustrated their importance, and provided actionable steps to actualize them, it is clear that trust is not a mere abstract ideal but a tangible, vital asset that can enhance performance, innovation, and employee satisfaction.

By weaving these elements into your daily interactions and decision-making processes, you can transform your work environment into a place where trust is not just expected but passionately cultivated.

This transformation will not only enhance your relationships with colleagues but also elevate the entire organizational culture. You'll contribute to a cohesive, transparent, and empowering workplace, where everyone, including you, can thrive more effectively.

TRUST QUESTION

· · · · · · · · · · · · · · · ·

How much does a demonstration of integrity, or lack thereof, impact your colleague's ability to trust you?

We often hear that integrity is foundational to building trust, but how do daily, seemingly minor actions or omissions affect this dynamic? Here are everyday scenarios showcasing how a demonstration of integrity breeds trust, while a lack thereof plants seeds of distrust:

Reporting Errors:

- **Trust:** Promptly admitting to a mistake in a monthly report before it affects the team.

- **Distrust:** Choosing to hide the error, hoping no one will notice.

Handling Confidential Information:

- **Trust:** Keeping a colleague's disclosed personal situation confidential, even when not explicitly asked to.

- **Distrust:** Sharing sensitive information about a colleague in a team chat, underestimating its personal value.

Meeting Deadlines:

- **Trust:** Communicating proactively about a potential delay in a shared task, giving your colleague time to adjust.

- **Distrust:** Repeatedly missing deadlines without forewarning, causing your colleague to scramble at the last minute.

Supporting Each Other:

- **Trust:** Publicly crediting a colleague for their idea that contributed to a project's success.

- **Distrust:** Taking full credit or neglecting to share credit for a project's success when it was a collaborative effort.

Managing Workload:

- **Trust:** Volunteering to help a swamped colleague with their workload without being prompted.

- **Distrust:** Assuming your colleague has it all under control and they will ask if they need help.

Acknowledging Input:

- **Trust:** Acknowledging receipt and thanking a colleague for their input on a document even if no major changes were made based on it.

- **Distrust:** Ignoring a colleague's contribution, making them feel undervalued and hesitant to contribute in the future.

Each example underscores small yet profound ways integrity, or the lack thereof, can subtly influence the fabric of trust within a team. It's clear that integrity is not just about the monumental moments but is often most meaningful in the everyday.

ARE YOU INADVERTENTLY ERODING TRUST?

Trust is delicate, taking time to build but moments to destroy. This chapter delves into the understated and often unintentional behaviors that might be quietly undermining the trust you share with your colleagues. Recognizing these pitfalls is crucial, and by actively steering clear of them, you have the ability to not only cement but also deepen and reinforce the fabric of trust in your professional relationships.

Pitfalls That Dent Trust

As you explore the pitfalls outlined in this chapter, take the opportunity to reflect on your own actions. This isn't about feeling judged; it's about gaining awareness. By understanding these behaviors, you can actively work to avoid them and enhance the trust with your colleagues moving forward.

The Incomplete Picture

. . . .

WHEN INFORMATION IS SCARCE, OUTDATED, OR INCOMPLETE, IT NATURALLY BREEDS UNCERTAINTY AND SKEPTICISM

. . . .

Withholding information, intentionally or not, fuels doubt and distrust. When critical updates, comprehensive context, or essential insights are absent, it feels like trying to complete a puzzle with pieces missing.

By ensuring that communication is inclusive, where every pertinent detail is shared transparently, you not only foster a cohesive, collaborative atmosphere but also affirm to your coworkers their valued position in your eyes.

Such inclusivity in sharing knowledge and updates underscores trust, reinforcing everyone's conviction that they are an integral part of the team's success. Transparency should be the cornerstone of your interactions, allowing for a mutual exchange of ideas that bolsters trust and collaboration.

Consider whether you might be inadvertently creating situations like the following, where withholding information can unintentionally undermine trust:

"I was asked to collaborate with John on a critical document due last week. Unfortunately, John delayed sharing crucial information about changes the client wanted until the day before the deadline. I was forced to work through the night to work these changes into our final draft."

"I really wish my colleague would loop me in on the full strategy for our project. More often than not, I'm left trying to fill in the blanks, which makes it hard to determine the best path of action when I only see part of the picture."

"I constantly find myself at a disadvantage during team meetings. It seems like Sarah selectively disseminates updates from leadership to certain team members while leaving others, including myself, in the dark. This leaves me looking unprepared in front the team."

"It's frustrating when I receive project updates from Tim in bits and pieces. He'll mention something crucial, as if it's a casual afterthought, which should've been brought to my attention weeks ago."

The Sea of Endless Corrections

. . . .

WHEN FEEDBACK BECOMES A STREAM OF WHAT'S WRONG WITHOUT RECOGNIZING WHAT'S RIGHT, IT UNDERMINES CONFIDENCE AND TRUST.

. . . .

Feedback should be a guidepost, not a gauntlet. A barrage of critiques, particularly if nitpicking or stylistic rather than substantive, can become overwhelming. Such excessive focus on faults without an equal if not greater focus on achievements and strengths can greatly undermine a person's confidence and the trust they place in your leadership or partnership.

Embracing a balanced feedback loop, which celebrates correctness as much as it constructively critiques, creates an environment where trust flourishes. Guiding with kindness and a genuine interest in each other's development nurtures a stronger, more resilient bond of mutual respect and trust. This balanced approach ensures feedback is a tool for empowerment rather than a weapon that erodes trust.

Reflect on these examples to see if you might be unknowingly deflating trust by focusing excessively on minor errors or preferences:

"Every time I send a draft over to Jeremy, it comes back drowning in red ink. It's not just the critical changes; it's everything, down to the most inconsequential details. It's like nothing I do is ever up to his standard, which is both exhausting and demoralizing."

"Working with Max is exhausting; he thinks his barrage of 'suggestions' for every document are helpful when in reality it's just frustrating. It feels less like support and more like an undermining of my expertise and confidence in my work."

"Laura's feedback always zeroes in on the negatives, completely glossing over what was done well. It's like walking on eggshells, knowing that no matter the effort, the focus will be on flaws rather than positives."

"Jen rarely voices her concerns directly but communicates her dissatisfaction through short, vague responses and minimal interaction with my ideas. This passive disapproval from a colleague makes me feel like I'm alone on an island."

The Magnifying Glass Mandate

. . . .

THE INSIDIOUS NATURE OF MICROMANAGEMENT NOT ONLY DEMONSTRATES A LACK OF TRUST IN TEAM MEMBERS' ABILITIES BUT ALSO SMOTHERS CREATIVITY AND INITIATIVE.

. . . .

When oversight becomes overbearing, you're not just controlling—you're signaling distrust. The antithesis of micromanagement is empowerment—giving colleagues the room to breathe, create, and take ownership of their work. By stepping back and entrusting your colleague to run with the task, you allow them the space to innovate and grow, thereby signaling your confidence in their capabilities.

Such empowerment leads to a more vibrant, dynamic work environment where trust is the foundation supporting collaboration and creativity. The transition from oversight to insight embodies a belief in people's potential and their capacity to excel when given faith and freedom. This change fosters a culture where trust is built on the pillars of freedom, respect, and mutual understanding.

These scenarios might help you identify if you are unintentionally stifling creativity and trust through micromanagement:

"Kevin nitpicks every detail of my work, down to the most minute aspects. It feels like he's constantly breathing down my neck; I can't even write an email without him wanting to check it first."

"Every time I make a decision, no matter how small, Elise insists on revisiting and analyzing it in excruciating detail. It's as though she's questioning every call I make, which makes me now second-guess myself all the time."

"For every project, Tom insists on being CC'd on all emails, even those that don't require his input. This constant surveillance feels less like guidance and more like a lack of trust in my capabilities."

"Rachel, my peer, often tries to dictate how I should complete my tasks. Her incessant meddling disrupts my workflow and makes simple tasks feel like team projects. I find myself spending more time appeasing her than focusing on the actual work at hand."

The Disappearing Act

··

IF REACHING YOU IS LIKE FINDING A NEEDLE IN A HAYSTACK, YOUR COLLEAGUES MAY FEEL NEGLECTED OR SECOND TIER.

··

Consistency in availability and responsiveness is crucial in nurturing trust with your teammates. Inconsistencies, delays, or a general lack of presence can leave your colleagues feeling undervalued and isolated, questioning their importance within the team. By prioritizing accessibility and timely responses, you communicate respect and appreciation for their efforts and time.

Ensuring that you are consistently present—both physically and virtually—demonstrates a steadfast commitment to supporting your colleagues, reinforcing the trust they place in you day after day. Such a presence, in turn, strengthens the fabric of your relationships, weaving a tighter knit of collective trust and respect.

Review these examples to determine if your lack of consistent presence might be inadvertently reducing the trust your colleagues place in you:

"Jane takes so long to respond to my messages, even on time-sensitive matters, that I'm forced into the uncomfortable role of constant follow-up. It makes me feel like a nag when all I'm trying to do is keep our work moving forward."

"Liam always says, 'I'm here if you have any questions,' but it's as if he vanishes into thin air the moment I try to take him up on his offer. He's always tied up in something else, making it nearly impossible to get the guidance I need."

"Every time I need Sam's feedback on a joint project, he is suddenly unavailable. His unresponsiveness leaves me hanging, forced to stall our progress or make decisions single-handedly."

"Alex is great at the kickoff of projects, full of ideas and enthusiasm. However, as we progress, his involvement fades because he gets involved in the next new thing. It is a struggle to keep him committed."

The Absent Appreciation

. . . .

A FAILURE TO ACKNOWLEDGE THE HARD WORK, EFFORT, AND SACRIFICES OF COLLEAGUES NOT ONLY DAMPENS MORALE BUT SIGNIFICANTLY ERODES TRUST.

. . . .

Feeling seen is just as important as being seen. Overlooking the hard work, dedication, and accomplishments of colleagues does more than dampen spirits; it gradually erodes the bedrock of trust that relationships are built upon. Acts of recognition, whether through public acknowledgment, personal notes of thanks, or even small tokens of appreciation, can significantly enhance a culture of trust and mutual respect.

By making appreciation a consistent practice rather than an occasional gesture, you foster an environment where everyone feels seen, valued, and motivated. These acts of acknowledgement validate the efforts of each individual, strengthening the trust between you and cultivating a more vibrant, supportive team dynamic.

Consider these situations to assess if you might be failing to adequately recognize and appreciate the efforts of others, thereby impacting trust and engagement:

"After spending countless evenings perfecting the document, all I received from Amy was a document full of redlines. No feedback, no acknowledgement of the effort it took to draft it under such a tight deadline. Just silent corrections."

"I rearranged my entire weekend to help Mark compile the necessary research for an urgent client request. Come Monday, not only was there no mention of my contribution in the team update email, but there was also no word of thanks privately."

"I spent considerable effort reworking a document after Peter's feedback. After sending him the updated piece, he simply said 'Thank you.' Nothing else."

"When Sophie's workload became overwhelming, I voluntarily picked up several tasks to keep the project on track. Once the crunch passed, Sophie never acknowledged my extra support; it was business as usual."

The Case of the Missing Why's

WITHOUT THE 'WHY' TO ANCHOR THE 'WHAT', ACTIONS CAN SEEM HOLLOW, AND TRUST MAY FALTER.

People rally behind an effort they understand. Take the time to elucidate the reasons behind directions and choices. When colleagues see the bigger picture and know how their work makes a difference, trust grows alongside commitment and motivation.

By openly sharing the rationale behind decisions, the impact of individual contributions, and the overarching goals, you anchor colleagues' work in meaningful context. This transparency cultivates deeper personal trust as each colleague recognizes the significance of their role and its direct impact on shared objectives. Such understanding reinforces trust and builds a bridge of mutual respect that underpins collaboration and collective achievement.

These examples will help you see if you might be omitting the 'why' behind actions, potentially leading to disconnected and distrustful team members:

"When Emily asks me to take on an assignment, she never explains how they fit into the larger strategy of the project. It's like being asked to solve a puzzle without the cover of the box."

"I spent hours drafting detailed client memos based on the template Rob provided, only to later discover that he had completely revised them without telling me why or giving any feedback."

"Lia asked me to help her analyze several datasets without telling me what specific problem we were trying to solve. This lack of context turned my task into a guessing game, significantly complicating my work and leaving me to navigate in the dark."

"Whenever I ask for the rationale behind new approaches Steve introduces, he brushes off my questions without providing answers. This not only leaves me puzzled but also feeling disrespected and dismissed."

Understanding the nuanced behaviors that erode trust, ranging from withholding vital information to failing to show appreciation, highlights the need for introspection and change in your actions and interactions. Emphasizing transparency, balanced feedback, empowerment, consistent presence, and recognition goes a long way in not only mending but fortifying the bonds of trust.

Moreover, providing the 'why' behind actions ensures that everyone feels connected and valued, crucial for fostering a collaborative and trusting environment. Reflecting on these aspects and making conscious efforts to address them can lead to stronger, more resilient professional relationships, where trust is not just rebuilt but thrives.

TRUST QUESTION

· · · · · · · · · · · · · · · ·

Does a returned document of redlines without any feedback breed trust or skepticism?

For many, encountering a document returned with redlines is just another day at the office. It's a norm—a quick way to communicate revisions without clogging the workflow. But here's something vital to consider: In the long term, or where relationships are yet to be cemented, a redlined document, devoid of any verbal discussion, can gradually elevate skepticism and erode the foundation of trust.

Not providing feedback alongside redlines is a missed opportunity, especially when we talk about nurturing trust between colleagues. Why is this the case?

- **Human Aspect:** Documents don't exist in isolation; they're the product of someone's thoughts, effort, and time. A solely redlined return can seem dismissive of this human aspect, potentially leading the author to feel undervalued and overlooked.

- **Opportunity for Growth:** Constructive feedback is a cornerstone of professional development. By skipping the chance to explain the reasoning behind changes or suggestions, you forfeit an opportunity to contribute to your colleague's' growth and, by extension, the team's evolution.

- **Communication & Understanding:** Trust thrives in an environment of open communication. Clear, constructive feedback fosters a better understanding between colleagues, bridging the gap between expectation and execution. Without this, misunderstandings become more likely, and with them, skepticism can grow.

- **Collaboration:** The essence of collaboration is working together toward a common goal, and trust is its lifeblood. A redlined document without feedback may create a barrier to this collaboration, implying a directive rather than a discussion.

- **Perception of Feedback:** Feedback, in its ideal form, is viewed as a gift. However, a barrage of unexplained redlines can make it feel more like criticism, shifting the perception of feedback from being helpful to punitive.

So, where does this leave you?

Not all redlines are created equal, and not every instance requires an in-depth critique. However, in fostering a workplace culture where trust prevails, it's crucial you don't overlook the power of pairing those redlines with constructive, explanatory information. This approach not only enhances the document at hand but also fortifies the professional relationship between you and your colleague.

In other words, the next time you're about to return a document with changes, consider adding a layer of commentary.

It could be as simple as a few words explaining a particular edit or a general comment on areas of improvement. This gesture can transform the redline process from a potential skepticism inducer into a trust-building tool, cementing the foundations of a collaborative and resilient relationship.

HOW DO YOU TRUST WHEN OUT OF SIGHT?

In the traditional office setting, where colleagues share a physical space day in and out, the elements of trust are often woven through the fabric of daily interactions, spontaneous conversations, and those serendipitous moments that occur beside the water cooler or in the break room.

This constant visibility and face-to-face communication allow trust to build almost organically, nurtured by the nuances of body language, vocal tone, and immediate feedback. It's in these everyday exchanges that a shared lunch or a quick chat about weekend plans can subtly reinforce the reliability and predictability between team members, laying a strong foundation for professional trust.

However, in today's evolving work environment, where hybrid models and remote workspaces are becoming more common, maintaining and building trust among colleagues who may rarely, if ever, share physical space presents unique challenges. The question arises: How do you trust when out of sight?

Without the luxury of physical presence, we lose the informal, often impromptu indicators of trustworthiness and commitment we take for granted in conventional settings. Trust must now be cultivated through different means, necessitating intentional actions and communication strategies that bridge the physical divide. This shift requires not only a reimagining of communication channels but also a deeper understanding of trust itself—how it's built, maintained, and sometimes repaired.

TRUST MUST NOW BE CULTIVATED THROUGH DIFFERENT MEANS, NECESSITATING INTENTIONAL ACTIONS AND COMMUNICATION STRATEGIES THAT BRIDGE THE PHYSICAL DIVIDE.

To navigate this new landscape, professionals must lean heavily on the principles of transparency, consistent communication, and empathy. Virtual meetings, regular check-ins, and clear project updates become more than just items on a to-do list; they are vital lifelines that maintain the flow of trust.

Furthermore, the empathy we might naturally extend in person—acknowledging a challenging workload, recognizing a job well done, or offering support during a tough day—needs to be consciously translated into our digital interactions. The art of building trust in a hybrid or fully remote environment also involves respecting boundaries, honoring commitments, and being responsive, which collectively signal reliability and build confidence among distant colleagues.

This shift calls for a reassessment of how trust foundations are laid and sustained, demanding innovation in how we connect, share, and collaborate when the office is no longer just a place we go to but a space we create across distances.

As we transition from water cooler chats to instant messages, from conference room meetings to Zoom calls, the essence of trust remains unchanged—it's the methods we employ that transform. In adapting to these methods, the invisible threads that tie team members together grow stronger, proving that trust, even when out of sight, need not be out of mind.

Potential Challenges

Without the physical proximity and the natural day-to-day interactions office life provides, certain issues may surface, affecting coworker dynamics and overall productivity. Here we outline some of the most pressing challenges that remote work may cultivate, which can impede the natural trust-building process and collaborative spirit among colleagues.

Communication Misunderstandings: In a virtual work environment, communication is primarily reliant on digital tools, which leaves room for misinterpretations and missed nuances inherent in face-to-face interactions. Ambiguities in written communication and limited exposure to colleagues' non-verbal cues (like tone and facial expressions) can lead to misunderstandings or assumptions that may challenge the trust between colleagues.

Lack of Shared Experiences: Trust is often built on shared experiences and informal interactions that happen organically in a physical office. Remote work strips away opportunities for spontaneous coffee breaks or quick desk chats, which can help build personal connections and mutual understanding. Without these casual interactions, building relational trust can be significantly more difficult.

Performance Visibility Issues: In remote setups, it's challenging to clearly see or appreciate the efforts and contributions of colleagues. This lack of visibility can lead to perceptions of unequal effort or commitment, possibly breeding mistrust or doubts about a colleague's dedication or efficiency. Regular updates and transparent workflows are essential but sometimes insufficient to fully convey the extent of an individual's contributions.

Hesitancy in Virtual Participation: The shift to digital meeting platforms can often result in participants feeling less inclined to speak up or share their opinions due to the impersonal nature of the interaction. Additionally, some individuals may consistently choose not to use their cameras during video calls, leading to a lack of visual presence. This reduction in active participation and personal visibility can hinder the development of trust and genuine connections, as it's challenging to build rapport with colleagues who seem distant or disengaged.

Slow Response Cycles: In remote work environments, the immediacy of feedback found in an office setting is often missing. Delays in receiving responses to inquiries, feedback on work, or approval for decisions can lead to frustration and a sense of isolation among colleagues. Over time, these delays can erode trust, as team members may feel their contributions are overlooked or undervalued.

What to Do Instead

With a clear understanding of the issues that remote work can bring, it's time to arm yourself with strategies to overcome them. Here are some tactics that can help you navigate these challenges effectively, enabling you to build trust and cultivate stronger, more collaborative relationships with your colleagues, no matter your location.

1. **Clarify Your Messages:** Always be precise and clear in your communications, providing necessary details to avoid misunderstandings. This includes using bullet points or numbered lists for complex ideas and summarizing long discussions to ensure key points are captured.

2. **Seek Understanding:** Don't hesitate to ask for additional information to ensure you have the right context if something in a communication is unclear.

Phrase your questions positively and constructively to foster an environment of open dialogue.

3. **Participate Actively in Check-ins:** Engage proactively in regular team meetings by sharing updates and raising concerns. This shows that you are involved and interested, and it encourages others to share as well, fostering a two-way communication channel.

4. **Join Virtual Social Events:** Participate in virtual social activities to build rapport with your colleagues. Activities like virtual games, coffee chats, or education webinar viewings can help create shared experiences that bind the team together.

5. **Share Personal Insights:** During team calls, share brief personal news or stories when appropriate to strengthen connections. Sharing appropriate and respectful anecdotes from your life can humanize the virtual work environment and bring warmth to digital interactions.

6. **Acknowledge Others' Efforts:** Regularly express appreciation for your teammates' work during calls or through messages. A simple acknowledgment can go a long way in making others feel valued and seen, which can boost morale and trust.

7. **Keep Team Members Updated:** Proactively share updates on your projects to keep your contributions visible. Regular updates prevent misunderstandings about workload or progress and help demonstrate ongoing commitment to the team's goals.

8. **Encourage and Practice Camera Use:** Turn on your camera during meetings and encourage others to do the same to foster a more connected experience. When your camera is on, it also motivates others to engage visually, which can lead to more effective and personable interactions.

9. **Respond Promptly:** Aim to reply to communications promptly or update the team if a delay is expected. Setting the expectation of when you will respond helps manage your colleagues' expectations and minimizes misinterpretations regarding work urgency.

10. **Utilize Collaborative Tools Effectively:** Actively use shared platforms for tasks and projects to ensure everyone can see your progress and contributions. Engaging with these tools not only keeps your work transparent but also helps you stay organized and responsive to team needs.

11. **Ask for Feedback:** Regularly request feedback on your work to demonstrate openness to improvement. This proactive approach can help you refine your performance and illustrates your commitment to collaborative growth.

12. **Engage in One-on-One Conversations:** Reach out for individual chats with colleagues to address specific issues or deepen relationships. Personal conversations can provide a more comfortable space to express thoughts and foster strong individual ties within the team.

13. **Promote Open Communication:** Encourage open and honest communication by being receptive and respectful when others share their thoughts or concerns. This helps to create a safe environment for expression, which is essential for building trust and ensuring all team members feel heard and supported.

14. **Support Flexibility in Work:** Recognize and support the need for flexible work hours among team members, understanding that remote work can come with varying domestic responsibilities. Empathy toward your colleagues' schedules can lead to more thoughtful planning and collaboration.

15. **Offer Flexible Meeting Options:** When scheduling meetings, provide multiple time options or alternate meeting methods, such as chat or collaborative documents, to accommodate different preferences and time zones. This approach demonstrates consideration for your colleagues' needs and promotes inclusivity within a distributed team.

Throughout this chapter, we've explored the complexities and nuances of maintaining and building trust in workplace environments where traditional face-to-face interactions are often replaced by digital communication. The shift from a physical office space to remote or hybrid settings poses real challenges in fostering trust, but it also opens a plethora of opportunities to rethink and enhance how we connect with one another.

By adopting these strategies, you can build resilient relationships with colleagues that not only adapt to the challenges posed by remote work but also thrive within them. It is through deliberate and authentic interactions that teammates can surmount geographical barriers, ensuring that trust remains steadfast—visible and impactful, even when your team members are out of sight.

TRUST QUESTION

· · · · · · · · · · · · · · · · ·

Have you ever been left out of the loop, rushing to fill in the blanks on a project at the last minute? How does being informed (or not) affect your trust in colleagues?

Information is both currency and cornerstone, shaping your ability to proceed, pivot, and predict. Yet, the granularity of being 'in the loop' or conspicuously 'out' can dramatically alter trust dynamics between colleagues. Consider these scenarios:

Proactive Updates vs. Silence: Being regularly updated by a colleague on project progress fosters a sense of collaboration and reliability. Conversely, discovering updates through a third party or very late in the process can seed doubts about the transparency and intentions of our teammates.

Open Invitations vs. Closed Doors: When a colleague extends an invitation to a project meeting, even as an observer, it creates an atmosphere of inclusivity and respect. Finding out about these meetings after the fact can make one feel undervalued and isolated.

Shared Challenges vs. Solo Battles: A colleague who openly shares challenges or roadblocks in a project allows for shared problem-solving and strengthens trust in their honesty. On the flip side, learning about problems after they've caused wider issues can breed mistrust about a colleague's competence or willingness to collaborate.

Mutual Learning vs. Information Hoarding: Sharing insights or learnings from a project can enrich a team's knowledge and promote a culture of growth. Being kept out of such knowledge sharing can lead to feelings of being sidelined and question a colleague's commitment to team success.

These everyday scenarios underscore how essential transparency, communication, and inclusivity are in nurturing trust. This isn't only about project success; it's about creating a workplace culture that values and respects every contribution.

HOW DO YOU ASSESS THE IMPACT OF MISTAKES?

Mistakes in the workplace are inevitable. However, not all mistakes have the same repercussions. Understanding and assessing these impacts effectively is crucial for maintaining trust and harmony within professional relationships.

Effective management of mistakes is often more indicative of your character and capabilities than the mistakes themselves. It is key to discern whether a mistake is a "minor misstep," which might be easily rectified and forgiven, or if it is a "critical blunder," potentially causing lasting damage to trust.

Minor missteps are those small, often negligible errors that are part and parcel of everyday work life. These are the errors that, while momentarily setting back the flow of work, are easily rectified and carry little to no long-term consequences. They are seen as opportunities for quick learnings and adjustments without significant disruption.

- -

EFFECTIVE MANAGEMENT OF MISTAKES IS OFTEN MORE INDICATIVE OF YOUR CHARACTER AND CAPABILITIES THAN THE MISTAKES THEMSELVES.

- -

On the far other end lie critical blunders—severe mistakes that carry substantial repercussions. These are not just simple oversights but significant errors that can jeopardize the success of a project, damage professional relationships, or undermine trust within a team.

This chapter introduces the Trust Impact Matrix, which helps you to discern if a mistake is a minor misstep or a critical blunder. The matrix presents two dimensions: Severity and Conduct. This dual-dimensional approach allows for a comprehensive assessment of mistakes, providing a framework to not only measure the impact but also to guide the recovery process.

The Severity dimension assesses how the error affects outcomes, relationships, and reputation. It gauges the potential ripple effects ranging from negligible to catastrophic. On the other hand, the Conduct dimension examines the behavioral response to the mistake, including how quickly and effectively it is acknowledged, addressed, and rectified.

Each dimension is discussed in detail in the following sections, offering insights into their intricacies and implications. Handling errors with transparency, integrity, and a proactive attitude towards resolution can help mitigate negative impacts and even strengthen trust over time.

Dimension One: Severity

In the realm of assessing the aftermath of workplace mistakes, the dimension of Severity within the Trust Impact Matrix addresses the ramifications of the error. This component of the matrix identifies the seriousness of impact through three crucial sub-areas: Consequence, Visibility, and Reputation.

Consequence

The Consequence section looks at the direct results of a mistake, focusing on three main areas:

Cost: Determines if the error has caused a significant financial loss, which can impact how the mistake is handled.

Time: Checks whether correcting the error will take a lot of time, potentially affecting project schedules, productivity, and the possibility of further delays.

Relationships: Considers how the mistake might have damaged trust and professional relationships. Even one error can weaken trust, thereby requiring work to rebuild confidence in the partnership.

Visibility

Visibility focuses on the exposure level of the mistake, considering who has witnessed it and the importance of that audience:

- Analyzing if the mistake was noticeable by a wide range of individuals or confined to a smaller, perhaps more manageable, group. The broader the awareness, the greater the potential for reputational damage.

- Considering the significance of those who observed the mistake, especially critical stakeholders, which can amplify its perceived severity due to potential implications on career progression and team dynamics.

Reputation

The final sub-area, Reputation, examines the long-term implications for both individual and organizational standing in the wake of a mistake. It raises crucial questions about the lasting effects on professional images:

- How does the error tarnish (or not) the reputation of the person whose trust has been impacted? For example, if you ask a colleague to assist with a project and they make a mistake, how is your reputation affected?

- How much does the mistake might damage the organization's reputation for reliability and trust? Does it possibly affect relationships with clients and standing in the market?

The Severity section of the Trust Impact Matrix helps you measure how serious a workplace mistake is by looking at its consequences, who knows about it, and how it affects reputation. By considering these factors, you can figure out if a mistake is a minor misstep, easy to fix with little fallout, or a critical blunder with more significant effects, and then take the right steps to deal with it and move on.

Dimension Two: Conduct

The Conduct section of the Trust Impact Matrix focuses on how a person handles a mistake and how their actions affect trust with those around them. This area looks at three main qualities: Competence, Openness, and Empathy. How these qualities are demonstrated after a mistake can either help preserve trust or lead to its erosion. Essentially, it's about the behavior and responsibility shown during the resolution of the mistake.

Competence

This area looks at whether a person has the right skills for their job and if they're using those skills well:

- If someone keeps making mistakes or isn't doing their job well, it might make others question if they're right for the task or job. This could be because they lack the skills or aren't willing to learn and improve, which can really hurt trust.

- If a person doesn't get better at their job even after making mistakes, it can look like they don't care about growing or doing well, which can reduce trust from teammates and bosses.

Openness

This aspect evaluates how openly a person admits to their mistakes:

- Trust fades when someone fails to promptly reveal a mistake or tries to hide it. Being upfront and timely in communication is key to keeping trust intact.

- Covering up mistakes can suggest a person lacks integrity or responsibility, qualities crucial for trustworthy professional relationships.

Empathy

This element looks at how well a person understands and addresses the effects of their mistake on others:

- If someone does not recognize or respond to how their mistake affects their colleagues or the organization, it shows a lack of empathy. Ignoring the impact on the team's morale, workload, and goals can greatly reduce trust.

- On the other hand, showing concern and taking steps to fix the issue can ease tensions and help maintain trust. It indicates that the individual cares about their relationships and the team's overall success.

The Conduct section looks at how a person behaves and reacts after making a mistake, and how these actions can either lessen or worsen its effect on trust. Three key factors are important here: Competence, Openness, and Empathy. How well someone handles these areas after a mistake can make a big difference in maintaining or even increasing trust. The better someone deals with a mistake in these aspects, the more likely they are to keep or build trust.

The Matrix in Action

Let's dive into a practical example of using the Trust Impact Matrix in a workplace scenario. Consider a case where two colleagues, Sam and Chris, are working together on a project. Chris has missed a deadline, which might initially seem straightforward but can vary in seriousness depending on how they behave.

We'll investigate how different responses from Chris might rank on the Trust Impact Matrix, ranging from Level 1, a "minor misstep" that barely affects trust, to Level 5, a "critical blunder," which severely damages it. Equipped with this analysis, Sam will not only be able to address the mistake appropriately but also objectively determine the impact on his trust with Chris as well as the best path for repair.

1. Consequence

- **Level 1 behavior:** The missed deadline has nearly no impact on the project's timeline or quality. Chris has missed a minor internal deadline, but the overall project is still on track. No external commitments are affected.

- **Level 3 behavior:** Chris's missed deadline causes minor setbacks in the project timeline and necessitates some reorganization of tasks. The progress of the project may be slightly affected, and there could be a need for some extra effort to stay on track.

- **Level 5 behavior:** Chris's failure to meet the deadline causes the project to be delayed significantly, incurring additional costs, straining relationships with clients, and putting future opportunities at risk.

2. Visibility

- **Level 1 behavior:** The deadline was a personal milestone for Sam and has no external visibility. There's now awareness of the missed deadline by other team members or stakeholders.

- **Level 3 behavior:** The missed deadline becomes known to a few team members beyond Sam, leading to some concerns within the team, but it doesn't grow into a broader issue that reaches external stakeholders.

- **Level 5 behavior:** The missed deadline is highly visible and becomes a point of discussion among stakeholders, clients, and within the team, affecting perception and reputation of the team.

3. Reputation

- **Level 1 behavior:** The missed deadline doesn't cast any doubt on Chris's overall reliability or the team's reputation. It's seen as an outlier in an otherwise impeccable track record.

- **Level 3 behavior:** Chris's failure to meet the deadline raises some questions about his reliability among his immediate team members, but it is still generally assumed to be an exception rather than the norm for his overall performance.

- **Level 5 behavior:** The missed deadline seriously questions Chris's professionalism and reliability, damaging both his reputation and the team's standing with clients and within the organization.

4. Competence

- **Level 1 behavior:** Chris demonstrates a high level of skill and expertise throughout the project. The missed deadline is attributed to an unforeseen and uncontrollable event, not a lack of ability.

- **Level 3 behavior:** Chris's expertise is generally sound, but the missed deadline points to potential areas for improvement or better time management. He is willing to address these areas to avoid future issues.

- **Level 5 behavior:** Chris frequently misses deadlines due to apparent gaps in skills and knowledge necessary for the project. He shows no interest in improving or seeking help to address these shortcomings.

5. Openness

- **Level 1 behavior:** Chris immediately informs Sam about the potential to miss the deadline well in advance, explaining the situation, which allows them to adjust plans easily.

- **Level 3 behavior:** Chris informs Sam about the missed deadline shortly before it occurs, providing some notice but not enough time to effectively adjust plans without some level of disruption.

- **Level 5 behavior:** Chris tries to hide the missed deadline from Sam and other stakeholders, only admitting it when the consequences become too evident to conceal, eroding trust significantly.

6. Empathy

- **Level 1 behavior**: Chris acknowledges the impact of the missed deadline on Sam's workload and actively seeks ways to mitigate the consequences, demonstrating concern for Sam's stress and time.

- **Level 3 behavior:** Chris recognizes that the missed deadline has some consequences for Sam and expresses a willingness to help where he can, though his understanding of the emotional strain on Sam is not fully apparent.

- **Level 5 behavior:** Chris shows no regard for how the missed deadline affects Sam or the project, dismissing any concerns raised by Sam or others, indicating a lack of empathy.

By rating Chris's behavior in each of these areas from "1" to "5", Sam can determine the overall impact of the missed deadline on trust. He could even use the various levels as "scores." When adding up all six scores, a result under 10 suggests the incident is a "minor misstep" with negligible to minimal impact, between 11 and 20 indicates a medium impact, within 21 to 25 points towards a significant impact, and anything over 26 is a "critical blunder."

Ultimately, the ability to navigate post-mistake trust effectively is crucial to fostering a resilient and collaborative professional relationship, such as the dynamics between Chris and Sam.

When workplace mistakes are understood and handled appropriately, it ensures that trust, the bedrock of any successful colleague teaming, remains intact or is restored. This not only mitigates short-term damage but also guards against long-term reputational harm, ensuring a culture where individuals feel empowered to grow from their errors and foster robust interpersonal and organizational relationships.

- -

WHEN WORKPLACE MISTAKES ARE UNDERSTOOD AND HANDLED APPROPRIATELY, IT ENSURES THAT TRUST REMAINS INTACT OR IS RESTORED.

- -

TRUST QUESTION

· · · · · · · · · · · · · · · · ·

When asked by a colleague to take on a task without understanding its impact, are you more or less motivated?

In the rush of daily To-Do's, we often find ourselves juggling tasks, some clearer in purpose than others. But consider this—when a colleague hands off a task to you without explaining why it matters, how does that influence your motivation?

Understanding the **'why'** behind our work is not just motivational; it's transformational. Here are a few thoughts on how clarity (or lack thereof) might affect us:

Clarity Boosts Engagement: Knowing the purpose behind a task can transform it from a mere item on your to-do list to a mission. You're not just compiling data; you're aggregating insights to drive business decisions.

Transparency Fosters Collaboration: When a colleague shares the impact of a task, it opens the door for collaboration. You're encouraged to share ideas or propose solutions, knowing the broader context.

Purpose Drives Innovation: Understanding the impact of your actions can lead you to think outside the box. Rather than simply completing a task, you might find a more efficient, innovative way to achieve the desired outcome.

Lack of Insight Can Lead to Disconnection: On the flip side, tasks without explained purposes can feel mechanical, reducing motivation. It's like being a cog in the machine without seeing the whole.

Trust and Respect: When colleagues take the time to share the 'why', it demonstrates respect and trust in your capabilities and interest. This, in turn, deepens professional relationships and mutual respect.

Understanding the impact of our work does not just motivate us; it empowers and invests us in the outcome. It's a reminder that our contributions, no matter how small they might seem, are part of something bigger.

HOW DO YOU RESTORE TRUST AFTER IT CRUMBLES?

When trust is broken, it creates a chasm that, if left unaddressed, can undermine teamwork, productivity, and overall workplace harmony. Repairing trust is a delicate process that requires effort and commitment from both the person who caused the breach and the one who was wronged.

This chapter offers a comprehensive guide to navigating the complex process of trust restoration. It provides practical steps for both those who have been wronged and those who have caused the breach, emphasizing the importance of mutual effort and understanding. These strategies will help you rebuild a stronger, more resilient professional relationship.

When They Break Trust

Repairing trust after a breach is a delicate process and is often placed solely upon the shoulders of the one who caused the breach. However, successful restoration requires responsibilities for *both* parties involved.

For those who have been wronged, it's not just about waiting for the other to mend their ways; active involvement is crucial. Due to trust's reciprocal nature, repair necessitates an openness to forgiveness and a willingness to engage from both sides to promote understanding and reconnection.

This part of the process is inherently about giving the person who made the mistake an opportunity to explain themselves and demonstrate their commitment to change. It also means setting aside the natural inclination to hold onto grievances in favor of working towards a resolution.

Acknowledging the hurt and disappointment while staying focused on the bigger picture of rebuilding the relationship is key. This approach not only accelerates the repair but also contributes to a healthier, more resilient dynamic moving forward.

This dual commitment to transparency and reconciliation paves the way for constructive conversations that lay the groundwork for trust to be reestablished. Here's a detailed guide on how you can facilitate this healing process when a colleague has broken your trust.

. . . .

THIS DUAL COMMITMENT TO TRANSPARENCY AND RECONCILIATION PAVES THE WAY FOR CONSTRUCTIVE CONVERSATIONS THAT LAY THE GROUNDWORK FOR TRUST TO BE REESTABLISHED.

. . . .

Step 1: Identify the Causes of Mistrust

Trust is not simple or uniform; it's complex and varies depending on the situation. To effectively rebuild trust, it's essential to understand exactly which aspects of trust have been damaged. This means taking a close look at what specific actions or failures have led to feelings of distrust. For example, figure out whether the issue is a team member's habit of being late or whether it's about them submitting work that isn't accurate. It's important to be specific about what behaviors have caused distrust, so you can address them directly.

It's also crucial to separate actual evidence of problems from your own assumptions or biases. This means looking at the facts of what happened without letting personal feelings unfairly influence your judgment. If you're concerned about someone's dedication, focus on concrete instances where they let you down, rather than a conclusion that they are lazy and might not be trustworthy at all. This distinction matters because problems based on solid evidence can be discussed and potentially fixed, while a decree based on emotion and inference creates a chasm.

An objective look at the situation will help you target the real issues, making it easier to find solutions. If you know exactly what trust issues need to be addressed, conversations can be more focused and productive, leading to better chances of resolving the problems.

This approach lays a solid foundation for overcoming trust issues and moving toward a stronger, more trusting relationship.

Step 2: Deliver Constructive Feedback

When the causes of mistrust are identified, the next crucial stage is to calmly discuss it with your colleague. This conversation should be approached with the goal of mending and strengthening the relationship, not merely pointing out faults.

Discuss the specific behaviors that have led to trust issues so the feedback is clear and actionable. For example, instead of making a generalized judgment such as, "I can't trust your work," it's more effective to point out specific instances, like, "I've noticed some discrepancies in your reports, which makes it difficult for me to rely on the accuracy of the information you provide."

Delivering effective feedback is a skill that not only addresses existing issues but can also foster greater trust going forward. To achieve this, it's important to avoid language that might come across as accusatory or emotionally charged, which can lead to defensiveness.

Imagine Alex and Taylor are colleagues working on a project together, and Taylor has been struggling to meet agreed-upon deadlines, affecting their collective progress. Instead of Alex saying, "Every time your work is late, it throws off our entire schedule and holds everyone back," which might come off as dramatic and could make Taylor defensive, Alex could choose a more collaborative approach.

Alex might say, "I've noticed some of the project milestones have been missed, and I think it's impacting our timeline. Is there something I can do to help us stay on track? Maybe we can look at the workload or deadlines together and find a better strategy."

This method addresses the issue without pointing fingers at Taylor and suggests a team effort to find a solution, which can help maintain and even build trust between them.

Delivering feedback well is essential to the repair process. When planning this conversation, here are some additional tips to ensure it is productive and positive:

1. **Choose the Right Time and Setting:** Ensure that you choose a private, neutral setting for this discussion where you both feel comfortable. Timing is

also important; avoid times when either of you are under significant stress or time pressure.

2. **Be Specific and Objective:** Clearly explain what behaviors need to change and why. Use specific examples to illustrate your points. Being vague can create confusion and make it harder for the other person to address the issues.

3. **Be Present and Listen:** This conversation should be a two-way dialogue. Be prepared to listen as much as you talk. Encourage the other person to express their view and show empathy toward their situation. This can help defuse tension and create a more open exchange.

4. **Focus on the Future:** Frame the discussion around how improvements can be made moving forward. Offer possible solutions or ask for suggestions on how they think the issues can be resolved. This fosters a collaborative atmosphere.

5. **Express Confidence:** End the conversation by affirming your trust in their ability to change and improve the situation. Ending on a positive note can boost their morale and motivation.

By carefully structuring your feedback and maintaining a clear, respectful manner throughout the conversation, you can address sensitive issues without causing further damage to the relationship.

Step 3: Discern When You CAN Trust

The journey to restoring trust in a relationship, whether personal or professional, doesn't necessitate the immediate and complete reinstatement of trust across the board. It's okay to take it slowly, but what is important is to take the steps towards repair.

Begin by identifying specific situations or tasks where you do or can trust your colleague. Due to missed deadlines, you may not be able to trust their time management skills, but they do deliver high quality work. Therefore, you *can* trust their competence.

Continue to collaborate on tasks where you can rely on their high level of skills but break down tasks into smaller, more manageable ones that allow for closer tracking of progress or set up more frequent check-ins while doing the work.

By marrying trust in their skills with structured support in weak areas, a pathway for gradual restoration of full trust can be established, fostering a productive and reassuring working relationship.

Taking it step by step, focus on small wins. Celebrate instances of reliability and trustworthiness as they occur. This not only reinforces positive behavior but also contributes to the rebuilding of confidence on both sides.

Eventually, this careful, stepwise strategy helps to restore a sense of normalcy and trust in the relationship, thereby fostering a healthier, more resilient dynamic moving forward.

Step 4: Self-assess Your Own Possible Culpability

Trust is a two-way street, and it's critical to engage in self-reflection to understand if your own actions may have contributed to the degradation of trust in your interactions.

Consider a scenario where a colleague has missed a deadline. Did you explicitly state the importance of the due date and discuss what was required to meet it? Were you available when they had questions? Did you provide timely information so they could make the deadline?

Accepting your part in misunderstandings helps build a culture where everyone is willing to own up to their mistakes and learn from them. It means taking a hard look at your actions and making changes where needed.

This kind of self-reflection isn't just about figuring out where you went wrong; it's about genuinely living out honesty and transparency. By doing this, you not only prove you're trustworthy but also set a standard, encouraging others to act similarly.

Initiating conversations about trust issues, providing space and opportunities for the person to regain your trust, and introspecting about your own contributions to the problem—these steps lay down a robust framework for trust restoration. Remember, the key to rebuilding trust is a balanced approach where both parties actively participate in healing and re-establishing the relational foundation.

By following these steps, not only can you potentially restore the trust that was lost, but you might also strengthen the relationship to withstand future challenges, creating a deeper, more understanding partnership. Remember, in the delicate dance of trust, every step forward, no matter how small, is a leap toward a stronger bond.

When You Break Trust

Realizing that your own actions have led to a breakdown in trust can be a humbling experience. It's not uncommon to find yourself on this side of the equation, where perhaps errors made by you, intentionally or unintentionally, have caused others hassle and damage. Recognizing and accepting your role in breaking trust is the first step toward mending those bonds.

This realization is often accompanied by a mix of emotions, including guilt, regret, and even fear of the consequences. Such feelings are natural and indicative of a conscientious person who values the trust placed in them.

In a professional environment, where precise coordination and mutual reliance are paramount, the impact of these errors can ripple through teams and projects, magnifying the importance of swift and effective resolution.

Embarking on this journey of repair requires not just acknowledgment but also a genuine reflection on the actions that led to the breakdown. This process involves introspection, understanding the full scope of the impact your actions have had, and developing a clear plan to avoid such pitfalls in the future.

The key is to approach this situation not as a victim but as an active participant ready to make amends. This means being ready to listen, understand, and empathize with those affected by your actions. It's about taking responsibility, not just in words but through meaningful actions that demonstrate your commitment to restoring trust.

IT'S ABOUT TAKING RESPONSIBILITY, NOT JUST IN WORDS BUT THROUGH MEANINGFUL ACTIONS THAT DEMONSTRATE YOUR COMMITMENT TO RESTORING TRUST.

Below is a practical guide on how to move forward if you've made a mistake that has affected your teammate. These steps are designed to help you mend and strengthen the affected relationship.

To address and rectify a mistake effectively, follow these detailed steps that emphasize responsibility and proactive problem-solving:

1. Acknowledge or Apologize for the Mistake

Begin by openly recognizing your involvement in the mistake. If the fault lies with you, it's crucial to offer a genuine apology. This not only shows your integrity but also begins the dialogue about making amends.

Acknowledging your mistakes upfront can help to disarm any potential confrontation and demonstrates your commitment to transparency and ethical behavior.

2. Acknowledge the Impact of the Mistake

It's important not only to apologize but also to explicitly recognize how your actions have affected others. This step is vital as it shows your awareness of the consequences of your mistake beyond your immediate scope.

For example, if your error caused extra workload or stress, explicitly acknowledge it: "I realize that because of my oversight, you were forced to spend additional time to rectify it over the weekend, which I genuinely regret."

3. Own and Offer

After taking responsibility, it's crucial to initiate the next steps towards resolution. Propose specific, realistic solutions to mitigate the error and, whenever possible, offer alternatives.

This allows your colleague to choose from the options you provide, catering to their preference and thus, giving them a sense of control and involvement in the resolution process. It shows your proactivity and dedication to not only fixing the error but also to safeguarding their interests.

4. Share Prevention Strategies

If the mistake is likely to recur due to the nature of the task, outline specific preventative measures that can be implemented. This might include additional checks, enhanced training, or new guidelines to follow.

Sharing these strategies reflects your commitment to continuous improvement and helps to build confidence in your ability to manage and adapt to prevent future errors. It also encourages a culture of learning and safety within your team or organization.

Throughout this process, keep in mind that rebuilding trust is about creating a new, stronger foundation in your relationships. It requires ongoing commitment, transparency, and respect for the feelings of those you've crossed. By assuming a proactive and sincere approach, you can mend the bonds of trust and move forward more wisely and compassionately.

TRUST QUESTION

· · · · · · · · · · · · · · · · · · ·

**Was there a time when you successfully
rebuilt trust with a colleague after
a misunderstanding? What was
imperative to that rebuild?**

In your career, misunderstandings and miscommunications
are inevitable. However, the resilience of your professional
relationships is tested not by these challenges themselves,
but by how you navigate the journey back to mutual trust
and respect.

I recall a time when a significant misunderstanding with
a colleague put a project we were both passionate about at
risk. The mix-up stemmed from an email that was intended
to clarify roles but ended up causing confusion about responsibilities. Tensions escalated quickly, affecting not only
our collaboration but also the project's progress.

The key to rebuilding our trust involved several crucial
steps:

1. **Immediate Acknowledgement:** We acknowledged
   the misunderstanding swiftly without assigning
   blame. Recognizing the issue openly paved the way
   for a constructive conversation.

2. **Open Communication:** We dedicated time to sit
   down and discuss the misunderstanding openly and
   honestly. This was not a quick chat between tasks
   but a focused effort to understand each other's
   points of view.

3. **Apologizing Where Necessary:** Both of us took responsibility for our parts in the misunderstanding. A genuine apology can go a long way in healing professional relationships.

4. **Re-establishing Expectations:** Together, we revisited and clearly defined our expectations moving forward. This helped prevent similar issues and ensured we were aligned in our project goals.

5. **Reinforcing Trust Through Actions:** Trust is rebuilt in the small moments. Following the conversation, we made a concerted effort to demonstrate our commitment through reliability, consistent communication, and support for one another.

6. **Reflecting and Learning:** Finally, this experience became a learning opportunity. We reflected on what went wrong and how we can better prevent and handle potential misunderstandings in the future.

This incident taught me that trust is not just about believing in someone's abilities or intentions; it's also about the willingness to work through misunderstandings together, with integrity and openness. The concerted effort to repair our working relationship not only salvaged our project but also strengthened our professional bond, making us better collaborators.

ARE YOU NURTURING OR NEGLECTING TRUST WITH YOUR CLIENTS?

Trust is the linchpin of any successful client or customer relationship, serving as both the foundation and framework upon which long-term partnerships are built. It's the invisible thread that stitches together lasting partnerships, fostering environments where open dialogue, mutual respect, and shared success can flourish.

Yet, despite its acknowledged importance, broken trust remains a common narrative in purchaser relationships. This paradox raises a critical question: if the value of trust with customers is universally recognized, why is its breach or lack of care so prevalent?

The answer lies in the delicate and dynamic nature of trust itself. Building trust with clients and customers is not a one-time achievement; it's a continuous endeavor that demands vigilance, consistency, and authentic engagement. While no one intentionally tries to sabotage trust with clients, it's a more regular occurrence than many realize.

Trust can be easily bruised by unmet expectations, miscommunications, or even perceived indifference to client needs. In a world where businesses and professionals grapple with an ever-accelerating pace and intensifying competition, priorities may inadvertently shift—placing the fragile bond of trust at risk.

However, each instance of broken trust presents not just a challenge but also an opportunity—a chance to revisit your approach, to reevaluate the principles you value, and to reconstruct stronger, more resilient foundations of trust.

This chapter focuses on understanding trust in client relationships, why it breaks down, and how to rebuild it. By grasping the details of trust, professionals can handle their relationships more confidently, turning potential weaknesses into strengths and maintaining integrity.

. . . .

WHILE NO ONE INTENTIONALLY TRIES TO SABOTAGE TRUST WITH CLIENTS, IT'S A MORE REGULAR OCCURRENCE THAN MANY REALIZE.

. . . .

One note—some businesses refer to purchasers as clients and others as customers. For our purposes here, we will use both interchangeably to represent the buyer of your services or products.

The Fragility & Importance of Trust in Client Relationships

Trust, in the context of client relationships, isn't a static commodity but rather a living entity that requires nurturing. When trust is firmly in place, the level of client engagement naturally intensifies, paving the way for more open, effective, and collaborative interactions. Trust serves as an affirmation of both competence and character, profoundly influencing how service is perceived and implemented.

The dual aspect of trust—encompassing both professional capability and personal integrity—is critical. Clients need to have confidence not only in the skills and knowledge of their service providers but also in their morals and ethical standards. When either aspect is doubted, the foundation of the relationship begins to crumble, leading to reduced communication and cooperation, which can ultimately impact project outcomes and business success.

Moreover, the frailty of trust is highlighted by its vulnerability to various threats. Simple misunderstandings, misrepresentations, and even external pressures such as market instability or competitive forces can strain the bond between a customer and a professional. The real challenge lies in not only establishing trust but maintaining it through these adversities, demonstrating a consistency of purpose, transparency, and responsiveness.

CLIENTS NEED TO HAVE CONFIDENCE NOT ONLY IN THE SKILLS AND KNOWLEDGE OF THEIR SERVICE PROVIDERS BUT ALSO IN THEIR MORALS AND ETHICAL STANDARDS.

Conversely, in a trusting relationship, clients are more likely to engage deeply, take calculated risks, and embrace innovative solutions, knowing they are supported by a trusted advisor who has their best interests at heart. In such an environment, the mutual commitment to a shared vision propels both customer and professional towards not just individual goals, but a partnership that achieves collective excellence and success.

Therefore, understanding and upholding the subtle yet sturdy lattice of trust is not just beneficial but imperative for sustained success in client relationships. By continuously fostering trust through every interaction, professionals safeguard not only their current projects but also future opportunities and ongoing collaborations.

Trust in Every Interaction

Building on the understanding that trust in the client-business relationship is akin to a delicately interwoven lattice, it's important to reflect further on its fragility and the care it necessitates. As previously highlighted, the creation of this trust is a labor of patience and dedication, unfolding slowly through years of reliable interaction and integrity.

This perspective underscores the importance of nurturing trust with conscious effort, showcasing through examples how each interaction contributes to or detracts from the solid foundation on which successful and enduring client relationships are built.

Yet, it's crucial to recognize that breaches in trust, often resulting from inadvertent actions rather than deliberate intent, can swiftly unravel this intricate fabric. Embracing the wisdom that "trust takes years to build, seconds to break, and forever to repair," we delve into a detailed exploration of the behaviors that either strengthen or weaken this lattice of trust.

Highlighted below are behaviors and practices that either contribute to the construction of a resilient bond of trust or lead to its unfortunate deterioration, underscoring the pivotal role that every interaction plays in this dynamic.

Actions That Build Trust

Let's begin by focusing on the positive actions that serve as the building blocks of trust. These are practices through which you can demonstrate your commitment, expertise, and genuine interest in your clients' success, laying down the keystones for strong, long-lasting relationships.

Actions	Client perspective
1. Deliver on promises and commitments consistently.	"They've never missed a deadline. I can always rely on their punctuality."
2. Practice active listening to understand client needs and concerns fully.	"Every time I speak, I feel heard. They truly listen and understand my needs."
3. Demonstrate expertise and competence without overselling capabilities.	"Their team knows their stuff, and they've never tried to oversell me on something I don't need."
4. Provide regular, clear, and transparent communication.	"Their updates are regular and informative. I'm never in the dark about where things stand."
5. Admit mistakes openly and offering solutions to rectify them.	"They owned up to the error immediately and made it right, no questions asked."
6. Show genuine interest and investment in the client's success.	"It's clear they're as invested in this project as we are. Their enthusiasm is genuine."
7. Respect confidentiality and handling sensitive information with care.	"I trust them completely with our sensitive data. They've proven their integrity time and again."
8. Meet deadlines or communicate proactively if a delay is unavoidable.	"They let me know ahead of time if something's going to be late, which helps me manage my schedule."

Actions	Client perspective
9. Offer constructive feedback and guidance.	"Their advice has always been spot-on and has helped us grow."
10. Ensure consistency in the quality of work or service provided.	"The quality of their work never falters—it's consistently excellent."
11. Acknowledge and value the client's knowledge and opinions.	"They truly value my opinion, which makes for a great working relationship."
12. Be accessible and responsive to inquiries and feedback.	"Whenever I reach out, they're there. It's like they're an extension of our own team."
13. Demonstrate flexibility to accommodate changing needs and circumstances.	"They've been flexible with our changing needs, which has been a lifesaver."
14. Follow through with aftercare, ensuring client satisfaction post-delivery.	"Even after the job was done, they checked in to make sure wo're still satisfied."
15. Build a rapport and seek a personal connection without compromising professionalism.	"We've developed a really strong rapport. It makes difficult conversations much easier."

Actions That Erode Trust

While it's essential to recognize and cultivate behaviors that build trust, it's equally vital to be aware of actions that can undermine it. As we transition into examining these detrimental practices, remember the intricate balance of trust and the ease with which it can be disrupted, underscoring the importance of introspection and vigilance in avoiding these pitfalls.

Actions	Customer perspective
1. Fail to meet deadlines without explanation or notice.	"They keep missing deadlines and it's throwing our whole schedule off."
2. Make excuses or shifting blame when issues arise.	"Whenever there's an issue, they give excuses but never own the problem."
3. Overpromise and underdeliver on services or outcomes.	"They promised the moon, but what we got wasn't even close."
4. Withhold information or be less than transparent about challenges.	"I feel like they're not telling us the whole story about what's going on."
5. Show inconsistency in pricing, agreements, or quality of work.	"Why did the price suddenly change? That's not what we agreed on."
6. Be defensive, dismissive, or unresponsive to feedback or complaints.	"I've given them feedback before, but it feels like they just don't care."
7. Demonstrate a lack of preparedness or knowledge in meetings.	"They seemed unprepared for our last meeting, which was a waste of our time."
8. Breach confidentiality or mishandle sensitive information.	"I heard that our project details were disclosed. That's a huge breach of our trust."
9. Neglect the importance of the client's input or perspective.	"I gave them some input, and it's like they didn't even consider it."
10. Provide generic or non-tailored advice and solutions.	"Their solutions feel like they could apply to any company. There's nothing customized about what they do."
11. Ignore or minimize client communications and inquiries.	"It's like our emails and calls go into a black hole. I never know when I'll get a response."
12. Allow personal biases to influence professional judgment or interactions.	"I feel like their advice is biased and not in the best interest of our business."

Actions	Customer perspective
13. Fail to follow up or check in on progress and satisfaction.	"They never follow up, so I'm never sure if they actually care about the work they did for us."
14. Demonstrate a lack of enthusiasm or interest in the client's projects or success.	"It's like they're just going through the motions—there's no passion or interest."
15. Engage in unethical practices or cut corners at the expense of quality.	"Cutting corners just to save a buck isn't what we signed up for. We expected better."

Building trust with a client doesn't happen overnight; it grows step by step, over time. Small actions that show you're reliable and have good intentions, known as "trust deposits," are key to this process. Every time you have a positive interaction, no matter how small, it helps build a stronger, more trustworthy relationship. Recognize these moments as chances to make progress.

As trust builds, it turns into deep confidence through constant positive experiences. When clients notice that you're really listening and acting on their needs, the trust between you gets stronger. Remember, trust is about accumulating small wins that lead to a strong, trusting connection.

The Criticality of Empathy

Empathy, as described in the Elements of Trust, plays a central role in customer relations; it's all about putting yourself in the client's shoes to truly grasp what they're feeling. Getting a handle on their world—recognizing the stresses they face, what they're hoping to achieve, and the obstacles they encounter—is essential. When you understand your client on this level, you can offer service that's really suited to their unique situation.

. . . .

EMPATHY IS ALL ABOUT PUTTING YOURSELF IN THE CLIENT'S SHOES TO TRULY GRASP WHAT THEY'RE FEELING.

. . . .

You'll also be able to predict what they might need next, before even they do, making your service proactive rather than reactive. Plus, every time you communicate, you'll do so with a relevance and respect that resonates with their current experience. In everyday business, showing empathy means you're not just talking to your clients; you're listening and responding in a way that makes them feel heard, supported, and valued. This, in turn, builds trust and strengthens the relationship you have with them.

Empathy shapes your communication, ensuring it's not just the words you choose but also the way you express them that builds trust. This means you've got to listen well when clients bring their concerns to you, show them you understand where they're coming from, and give thoughtful, sincere responses.

When you're empathetic, you explain things in a way everyone can understand, leaving out the confusing jargon. It's all about making complex information easy and approachable. You're aiming to make your clients feel comfortable and clued-in, rather than out of their depth.

It's not just about the talking, though. Empathy means your whole demeanor—your tone and even your body language—shows you care and you're there to help. You're patient, letting clients express themselves fully, and you're there to reassure them.

Empathy also comes into play after your discussion. Following up shows you're still thinking about their needs and are ready to offer more help. It's these extra steps, and the simple, clear, and caring way you talk and act that build lasting trust and make your clients feel valued.

Reading and Reacting to the Warning Signs of Distrust

Clients may not always vocalize their feelings of distrust or dissatisfaction straightaway. Instead, they might exhibit certain behaviors or "clues" that their trust is waning. Recognizing these signs early allows for proactive measures to address and mitigate underlying concerns.

1. Reluctance to commit to timelines or next steps.

2. Infrequent or minimal communication, such as short, terse email responses.

3. Lack of enthusiasm or indifference when discussing projects or results.

4. Interrupting frequently or talking over you during discussions.

5. Canceling or rescheduling meetings more often than usual.

6. Withdrawal from previously agreed-upon plans or strategies.

7. Requesting to revisit or re-explain previously discussed topics.

8. Pointing out minor errors or issues more frequently.

9. Closed body language in meetings, such as crossed arms or lack of eye contact.

10. Not responding to follow-up calls or requests for feedback.

11. Expressing hesitation or doubt about your expertise or qualifications.

12. Seeking assurances or guarantees beyond the usual scope.

13. Showing resistance to providing necessary information or delaying in supplying it.

14. Bringing in advisors or third parties to review work unexpectedly.

15. Making comparisons to other service providers or competitors.

Once signs of distrust are identified, addressing them head-on can prevent further erosion of trust. This might involve initiating open and honest discussions to uncover and address concerns, providing additional reassurances or evidence to back recommendations, or simply being more present and available to the client. Each of these actions can help to rebuild confidence in the relationship.

Here are examples of conversation starters to help you jumpstart a restorative discussion.

Open Discussion on Concerns: "I've noticed some hesitation regarding our recent discussions. Can we talk about any concerns you might have?"

Feedback Inquiry: "I value your feedback to improve our collaboration. Is there anything specific you feel we could be doing better?"

Clarification Request: "In urgent situations, it's crucial we communicate effectively. Can you specify your preferred method of communication for these scenarios to ensure clarity and prompt response?"

Reaffirmation of Commitment: "I want to make sure we're on the same page and achieving your goals. Is there anything you'd like to change about how we're working together?"

Exploring Communication Preferences: "I've noticed our communication has lessened recently. How would you prefer we communicate, to ensure you're comfortable and informed?"

Project Status Check-in: "How are you feeling about the progress of our project so far? I'm here to address any thoughts or questions you might have."

Decision-Making Process: "When we discuss decisions and you seem unsure, I worry we might not be considering all your important factors. What would help to make these decisions feel more inclusive for you?"

Meeting Effectiveness: "I feel that our last meeting might not have met your expectations. How can we make our next session more effective?"

Encouraging Questions: "I appreciate when you ask probing questions—it helps me to understand your perspective better. What's on your mind that we haven't yet addressed?"

Building Mutual Trust: "Building a strong, trustful relationship is key for me. What steps can we take together to strengthen our partnership?"

Trust is the cornerstone of every successful client relationship, underpinning all interactions and engagements. This chapter has explored the vital role of trust, its delicate nature, and the continuous effort required to maintain it. We've seen that trust is not just built on professional competence but also on personal integrity and empathetic communication.

Actions that foster trust, like meeting commitments, active listening, and transparency, are essential for building strong, lasting client relationships. Conversely, behaviors that erode trust, such as failing to meet deadlines, shifting blame, and lack of transparency, can quickly damage these relationships. Recognizing the signs of waning trust and addressing them proactively is crucial to restoring and maintaining client confidence.

Ultimately, building trust is about making consistent, positive "trust deposits" through every interaction. Each small action contributes to a stronger, more resilient bond with clients, transforming potential vulnerabilities into pillars of strength and integrity. Through vigilance, consistency, and authentic engagement, you can navigate the complexities of your client relationships with confidence, ensuring long-term success and mutual growth.

TRUST QUESTION

· · · · · · · · · · · · · · · · · ·

**Have you ever felt invisible after pouring
your heart into a project? Is the omission
of appreciation and acknowledgement of
effort from a colleague just an oversight
or a deeper issue that impacts trust?**

There is nothing quite as disheartening in the professional
realm as dedicating oneself fully to a project, only to have
one's effort and contribution go unrecognized. It raises
an important question about the nature of work, recognition, and how these factors intertwine with trust between
colleagues.

Acknowledgment Fosters Trust: When colleagues acknowledge each other's efforts and contributions, even
if small, it's not just about giving credit where it is due.
It's about validating the individual's role in the team's
success, fostering a sense of belonging and trust.

Omission Can Signal Disregard: Continuous failure
to recognize effort can come off as disregard for a colleague's input and hard work. Over time, this perceived
slight can erode trust, making one question their value
within the team.

Appreciation as a Motivation Driver: On a brighter
note, appreciation and acknowledgment serve as significant motivators, encouraging individuals to continue

putting forth their best effort. It reassures us that our work is meaningful and impactful.

Trust, Respect, and Communication: The act of appreciating and acknowledging contributions isn't just about trust; it also ties into respect and open communication. A culture that promotes these values will see stronger, more cohesive teams.

Ensuring that every effort between colleagues is recognized and acknowledged becomes crucial in upholding a positive work dynamic. By actively appreciating each other's contributions, colleagues can strengthen their relationship, built on mutual trust and respect. This act of acknowledgment not only underlines the importance of each individual's role within a team but also serves as a fundamental element in fostering a collaborative and trust-filled working relationship.

HOW DO YOU FOSTER TRUST BELOW AND ABOVE?

Trust is often viewed as a vertical currency in the world of business, flowing between managers and their direct reports. Managers work to gain the trust of their direct reports, and team members strive to do the same with their higher-ups.

Initially in this book, we emphasized the importance of cultivating trust among peers because once you know how to build trust with colleagues, you can use those skills in any direction. Now, we are focusing on developing trust vertically, teaching how to build it with superiors and subordinates.

This chapter guides you through the intricacies of establishing trust with both your juniors and seniors. It's not just about building good relationships but about concrete tactics to foster trust throughout the hierarchy, making you an influential leader and a reliable team player.

Fostering Trust Below

Before we explore the crucial techniques for managing down, take this opportunity to assess your own skill in developing trust with your team members. This quiz will challenge you to identify the key actions that best foster trust with your direct reports. You can find the correct answers in the Appendix at the end of this chapter. Let's begin!

Question 1: You're leading a team meeting and discussing upcoming project changes that will significantly impact everyone's tasks. What is the most effective way to foster trust during this conversation?

    A) Provide detailed information and explain the reasoning behind the changes. Encourage team members to ask questions and express any concerns.

    B) Assure the team that everything is under control, and they do not need to worry about the specifics.

    C) Make quick decisions in the meeting to show decisiveness.

Question 2: A team member approaches you with an innovative idea that could potentially improve your current project but involves some risk. How should you respond to foster trust?

A) Thank them for their input but choose the route that you know is guaranteed to be effective.

B) Listen to the suggestion and tell them you'll think about it.

C) Acknowledge their idea, discuss the potential risks and benefits, and consider running a small test of the concept.

Question 3: One of your team members has consistently been turning in excellent work and going above and beyond in their tasks. What action fosters trust and shows your appreciation for their dedication?

A) Give a quick thank-you in the team meeting.

B) Provide specific praise for their contributions in a 1:1 check-in and consider rewards that match their efforts.

C) Make a mental note of their performance, planning to acknowledge it during their next performance review.

Question 4: Your team is undergoing a stressful period, with tight deadlines and high stakes. How can you maintain and foster trust amidst the pressure?

A) Keep concerns to yourself to avoid adding stress to the team.

B) Increase supervision to ensure everyone stays on task.

C) Hold a meeting to openly discuss current challenges, available support, and strategies to manage stress collectively.

Question 5: A team member has made a mistake that caused a minor setback. What approach builds trust while addressing the issue?

A) Use this mistake as a teachable moment and discuss it at the next team meeting to ensure it doesn't happen again.

B) Privately discuss the mistake, emphasize learning from it, and explore solutions together.

C) Provide reassurance to the team member that mistakes happen but be sure to note it on a future performance review.

Question 6: When planning the strategy for the upcoming project, you have several options that are possible. How do you foster trust through your decision-making process?

A) Decide yourself on the direction that seems best to you because that's your job as the manager.

B) Explain the possible directions to the team, seeking their input and weighing all options before making a decision.

C) Continue to research and develop the plan and present it to the team once you have it vetted and finalized.

Question 7: You recognize the value in personal and professional growth for your team members. What action best supports this while building trust?

A) Prioritize and make time for team members to attend relevant training, supporting their development goals actively.

B) Advocate team members independently seek out training opportunities as their schedule permits, emphasizing self-led growth.

C) Encourage participation in training sessions while also underscoring that work obligations take precedence, acknowledging that they may have to miss the training if you need them.

How did you score? Understanding and implementing these strategies is key to building a solid, trust-based relationship with your team members. Now, let's dive into these essential actions for fostering trust downwards.

7 Effective Actions for Managing Down

Successfully managing down requires a thoughtful approach to leadership—one that cultivates an environment of transparency, respect, and mutual trust. When team members feel valued and trusted by their managers, they're more likely to engage, perform, and contribute to a positive workplace culture.

. . . .

WHEN TEAM MEMBERS FEEL VALUED AND TRUSTED BY THEIR MANAGERS, THEY'RE MORE LIKELY TO ENGAGE, PERFORM, AND CONTRIBUTE TO A POSITIVE WORKPLACE CULTURE.

. . . .

As a manager of people, it's your responsibility to initiate this cycle of trust, creating a foundation that supports both individual and collective success. To guide you in this critical aspect of management, we've outlined seven effective actions or techniques designed to deepen the trust between you and your team members.

Here are seven effective actions or techniques that you can employ to foster trust with those who work for you:

Consistent and Open Communication

Prioritize clear, honest, and consistent communication. Keep team members informed about team goals, changes, and project statuses. Encourage open dialogue where team members feel comfortable sharing their ideas, concerns, and feedback.

Demonstrate Integrity and Reliability

Lead by example by acting with integrity. Follow through on promises and commitments. If circumstances change, communicate the reasons promptly and transparently. Consistency between what you say and what you do is key to building trust.

Involve Team Members in Decision Making

Seek input from team members on decisions that affect their work or the team's direction. This inclusion not only improves decision outcomes by incorporating diverse perspectives but also significantly increases team members' investment in and ownership of team goals and projects.

Acknowledge and Value Each Team Member's Contribution

Recognize and celebrate achievements and contributions of team members. Personalized acknowledgments show that you notice and value each individual's efforts, enhancing their sense of belonging and trust in your leadership.

Foster a Safe Environment for Taking Risks and Making Mistakes

Encourage innovation and learning by creating an environment where calculated risks are taken, and mistakes are viewed as opportunities for growth. This approach helps in building a culture of trust where team members feel supported and valued for their efforts to innovate and improve.

Invest in Personal and Professional Development

Show a genuine interest in the personal and professional growth of your team members. Support their development through mentoring, training, and providing challenging opportunities that stretch their skills and capabilities. This demonstrates your commitment to their success and well-being, further cementing trust.

Practice Empathy and Understanding

Make an effort to understand the challenges and pressures your team members face, both in and out of the workplace. Approach conversations with empathy and provide support where possible. Recognizing and addressing the human aspects of work fosters a deeper, trusting relationship.

Building trust with your team is essential for effective leadership. The discussed strategies highlight the importance of openness, support, and transparency in empowering your team and boosting morale.

By consistently employing these approaches and genuinely engaging with your team members, you foster an environment where trust thrives, leading to improved performance and a stronger, more cohesive team dynamic.

Fostering Trust Above

Continuing our exploration of trust within the organization, now let's focus on building trust upward. Before moving to specific strategies, take a moment to evaluate your current behaviors. These questions are designed to highlight key methods for strengthening trust with your supervisors and other higher-ups. You can find the correct answers in the Appendix at the end of this chapter. Ready to proceed? Let's go.

Question 1: You encounter a roadblock in your current project that will likely delay progress. How should you approach this with your manager?

A) Present the problem along with potential solutions to your manager as soon as possible.

B) Do want you can to try to fix it yourself.

C) Review the project schedule to see if there are upcoming tasks that can be adjusted to accommodate the delay before bringing it up with your manager.

Question 2: You've just completed a major project ahead of schedule. What should you do next?

A) Take a break since you've finished early.

B) Utilize the remaining time to start exploring and researching upcoming projects or initiatives you can contribute to.

C) Inform your manager promptly and detail the results.

Question 3: It's going to be hard work to get all tasks completed to deliver the project to the client on time. What do you do?

A) Rely on your manager to hand out assignments as they see fit.

B) Volunteer as much as possible, especially for the tasks that you think you can do efficiently.

C) Wait for others to take the lead and then offer support where needed.

Question 4: Your team is brainstorming ways to improve a work process. What's your best course of action?

A) Keep quiet, as change is not your responsibility.

B) Let others take the lead and follow along with their ideas.

C) Suggest innovative solutions and volunteer to help implement them.

Question 5: You mistakenly send a client outdated information that could potentially cause confusion. What should you do?

    A) Blame the error on a system glitch or a colleague.

    B) Rapidly send a corrected version. Since you found it so quickly, you don't see a need to inform your manager.

    C) Swiftly admit the mistake to your manager and discuss how to rectify the situation.

How did you fare? Recognizing and initiating these actions will assist in cultivating a strong, trust-based relationship with your manager. Now, let's delve into these seven essential actions for fostering trust upwards.

7 Effective Actions for Managing Up

Navigating the dynamics of trust with those above you in the organizational hierarchy demands a strategic and respectful approach. It entails demonstrating your reliability, competence, and commitment, which can significantly influence your superiors' willingness to trust and support you.

As someone who reports to higher-ups, it's imperative to actively engage in behaviors that reinforce your credibility and show your dedication to the organization's goals.

This section is dedicated to unraveling the key actions and techniques that can help you strengthen the trust from your superiors, ensuring a productive and harmonious working relationship.

. . . .

IT'S IMPERATIVE TO ACTIVELY ENGAGE IN BEHAVIORS THAT REINFORCE YOUR CREDIBILITY AND SHOW YOUR DEDICATION TO THE ORGANIZATION'S GOALS.

. . . .

Here are seven effective strategies you can implement to foster trust with your managers and senior leaders:

Perform Consistently: Deliver high-quality work consistently and meet deadlines reliably. Demonstrating your commitment and reliability through your performance is foundational to gaining your manager's trust.

Communicate Regularly: Keep your manager informed about your progress on projects and any challenges you face. Transparency is key to establishing a healthy and trustful working relationship.

Be Solution-Oriented: When problems arise, focus on solutions rather than just presenting problems.

Managers appreciate team members who can identify issues and offer constructive ways to address them.

Collaborate Effectively: Be a team player and collaborate well with others. When managers see that you contribute positively to team dynamics and projects, it reinforces their trust in your abilities and character.

Take Initiative: Go beyond what's expected by thinking strategically, volunteering for assignments and demonstrating a "can do it" attitude. This shows that you are invested in the success of the team and the business.

Admit Mistakes: If something goes wrong, own up to it promptly and present a plan to address the issue. Honesty in difficult times can strengthen trust considerably.

Seek Feedback: Actively ask for and be receptive to feedback. Show that you value your manager's insights and are eager to grow professionally based on their guidance.

Successfully managing up by recognizing and initiating these actions can significantly bolster the trust-based relationship with your manager, paving the way for a more fulfilling and progressive career.

Successfully navigating the complex dynamics of trust in organizational structures demands a genuine, strategic approach both in managing down and managing up the hierarchy. As leaders and team members actively engage in building trust through transparency, integrity, and collaboration, they lay the groundwork for a resilient, high-performing team dynamic.

The journey to fostering trust is a continuous process, requiring commitment, empathy, and a deep understanding of the needs and aspirations of both subordinates and superiors. By embodying the principles and actions outlined, you set a strong example. Engaging actively in these trust-building practices not only elevates your leadership and team dynamics but also positions you as a pivotal influencer in the growth and success of your organization.

Appendix

Managing Down Quiz Debrief

Building trust with individual team members is at the heart of leading effectively. Here's a debrief that explains each correct and incorrect answer for the "Managing Down" questions. Understanding the reasoning behind each correct and incorrect answer can help you refine your approach, promoting a more cohesive, motivated, and resilient team.

Question 1: You're leading a team meeting and discussing upcoming project changes that will significantly impact everyone's tasks. What is the most effective way to foster trust during this conversation?

- **Correct Answer (A): Providing detailed information and encouraging open communication is crucial for trust. It shows respect for the team's ability to understand complex issues and offers an opportunity for them to be heard.**

- Incorrect Answer (B): Simply assuring the team without providing details can breed suspicion or uncertainty. Team members may feel left out of important conversations or not fully trusted with the information.

- Incorrect Answer (C): Making quick decisions without team input can appear authoritarian and neglects the team's insights, which could harm trust and team cohesion.

Question 2: A team member approaches you with an innovative idea that could potentially improve your current project but involves some risk. How should you respond to foster trust?

- Incorrect Answer (A): Dismissing the idea without exploration may cause team members to feel undervalued and disincentivized to offer future suggestions.

- Incorrect Answer (B): Saying you'll think about it but not providing follow-up can be perceived as disingenuous, leading team members to distrust your responsiveness to their contributions.

- **Correct Answer (C): Acknowledging new ideas and discussing their potential demonstrates that you value innovation and are open to taking calculated risks. It encourages a culture of trust and creativity.**

Question 3: One of your team members has consistently been turning in excellent work and going above and beyond in their tasks. What action fosters trust and shows your appreciation for their dedication?

- Incorrect Answer (A): A quick thank-you in a public setting may not fully convey the depth of your appreciation and can be perceived as a lack of genuine acknowledgment.

- **Correct Answer (B): Individuals need to feel valued. Providing specific, meaningful praise during**

private interactions can significantly boost trust and show genuine appreciation.

- Incorrect Answer (C): Waiting until a performance review to recognize efforts can diminish the immediate impact of the praise and may leave the team member feeling unappreciated in the interim.

Question 4: Your team is undergoing a stressful period, with tight deadlines and high stakes. How can you maintain and foster trust amidst the pressure?

- Incorrect Answer (A): Keeping concerns to oneself can lead to a culture of secrecy and unease, which can erode trust within a team.

- Incorrect Answer (B): Increasing supervision can suggest a lack of confidence in the team's abilities and can contribute to a micro-management environment, rather than fostering trust.

- **Correct Answer (C): Openly discussing challenges provides transparency and relieves the pressure through collective problem solving, reinforcing a trusting environment.**

Question 5: A team member has made a mistake that caused a minor setback. What approach builds trust while addressing the issue?

- Incorrect Answer (A): Discussing individual failings in a group setting can be embarrassing and potentially diminish trust by creating fear of public reprimand.

- **Correct Answer (B): Discussing the mistake privately and focusing on growth and solutions respects the team member's dignity and strengthens trust by showing support.**

- Incorrect Answer (C): While reassurance is good, mentioning the mistake in a performance review without immediate discussion at the time of occurrence may lead to feelings of resentment and undermine trust.

Question 6: When planning the strategy for the upcoming project, you have several options that are possible. How do you foster trust through your decision-making process?

- Incorrect Answer (A): Deciding without team consultation may seem dismissive of their expertise and perspectives, potentially weakening trust.

- **Correct Answer (B): Actively involving the team in the decision-making process reassures them that their opinions are valued, building trust through collaboration.**

- Incorrect Answer (C): While polished plans are good, failing to involve the team in the development may cause them to feel disconnected and less invested.

Question 7: You recognize the value in personal and professional growth for your team members. What action best supports this while building trust?

- **Correct Answer (A): Actively supporting and facilitating training signifies that you are invested in your team's growth, strengthening trust by directly contributing to their development.**

- Incorrect Answer (B): Encouraging self-led training puts the onus solely on the team members and might imply that their growth is not a managerial priority, which could adversely affect trust.

- Incorrect Answer (C): Suggesting that training should be secondary to work responsibilities can send a message that personal growth is not genuinely supported, potentially diminishing trust.

Managing Up Quiz Debrief

Fostering trust with your manager is crucial for a successful and productive work relationship. Understanding how to effectively manage up can make all the difference in your career progression and day-to-day job satisfaction. Here's a detailed look at the correct and incorrect answers for the quiz, designed to help you enhance trust upwards in your workplace.

Question 1: You encounter a roadblock in your current project that will likely delay progress. How should you approach this with your manager?

- **Correct Answer (A): Presenting the problem alongside potential solutions to your manager as soon as possible demonstrates being proactive, responsible, and committed to transparency, which are key components of building trust.**

- Incorrect Answer (B): Attempting to fix the problem by yourself without keeping your manager informed may come across as avoiding sharing bad news, which can lead to a loss of trust should the situation worsen or become more complicated.

- Incorrect Answer (C): Reviewing and adjusting the project schedule before speaking with your manager postpones direct communication and could complicate the situation if delays become unmanageable, leading to a potential breakdown in trust due to perceived lack of openness.

Question 2: You've just completed a major project ahead of schedule. What should you do next?

- Incorrect Answer (A): Taking a break because you finished early could be misconstrued as complacency and a lack of ambition, negatively impacting your manager's trust in your dedication.

- Incorrect Answer (B): While utilizing the time to explore upcoming projects is proactive, not directly communicating your success with the completed task misses the opportunity to positively reinforce trust through immediate transparency and recognition of your achievements.

- **Correct Answer (C): Promptly informing your manager and outlining the completed project's results showcases your efficiency and reliability, thereby strengthening their trust in your capabilities and communication skills.**

Question 3: It's going to be hard work to get all tasks completed to deliver the project to the client on time. What do you do?

- Incorrect Answer (A): Relying solely on your manager to delegate assignments might suggest a lack of proactivity or engagement in the project's success, which could weaken your manager's trust in your self-motivation and leadership abilities.

- **Correct Answer (B): Volunteering as much as possible, particularly for tasks that align with your strengths, displays initiative and commitment, crucial traits for fostering trust with your manager.**

- Incorrect Answer (C): Waiting for others to take the lead before offering help reflects passivity and can undermine trust by creating an impression of disinterest or lack of confidence in driving project success.

Question 4: Your team is brainstorming ways to improve a work process. What's your best course of action?

- Incorrect Answer (A): Staying silent during the brainstorming process may suggest to your manager that you are uninterested or not invested in team success, which potentially erodes trust in your involvement and contribution.

- Incorrect Answer (B): Allowing others to lead without offering your ideas may result in missed opportunities to display leadership and creative problem-solving skills, key qualities for nurturing managerial trust.

- **Correct Answer (C): Actively suggesting innovative solutions and volunteering for implementation establishes you as a dedicated and resourceful team player, enhancing your manager's trust in your initiative and collaborative spirit.**

Question 5: You mistakenly send a client outdated information that could potentially cause confusion. What should you do?

- Incorrect Answer (A): Blaming the mistake on external factors like a system glitch or a colleague undermines trust by avoiding responsibility and not displaying the integrity expected of a trustworthy team member.

- Incorrect Answer (B): Correcting the information sent to the client without notifying your manager misses a critical chance to foster trust by ignoring the importance of full disclosure and collaborative problem-solving in managing errors.

- **Correct Answer (C): Immediately admitting the error to your manager and working together on a solution conveys honesty and accountability, reinforcing trust by demonstrating your integrity and commitment to rectifying mistakes.**

Successfully managing up by recognizing and initiating these actions can significantly bolster the trust-based relationship with your manager, paving the way for a more fulfilling and progressive career.

TRUST QUESTION

· · · · · · · · · · · · · · · · ·

Have you ever witnessed transparency in communication act as a catalyst for building stronger trust with a teammate? What was the impact?

Transparency in communication is less of an option and more a necessity in the professional world. It's the foundation upon which trust is built and nurtured among colleagues. Let's consider two scenarios that illustrate its profound impact:

What Not to Do – Concealing Information:
Picture a situation where one coworker withholds relevant information about a project, leaving another struggling or caught off-guard at a critical moment. Not only does this breed frustration and impede the project's progress, but it also erodes trust. Over time, this could cultivate a toxic environment where teammates are wary of one another, hampering collective growth and success.

What to Do – Open Communication and Collaboration:
Now, imagine another scenario. A team member is candid about a potential delay in their segment of a project, consulting their colleague well in advance. Not only does this foster open dialogue about potential solutions, it also strengthens trust, reinforcing that each team member has each other's back. This cultivates a nurturing and

cooperative team culture, boosting morale and productivity in the long run.

These examples illuminate the critical impact of transparency on building and maintaining trust within teams. "Honesty is the best policy" sounds cliché, but it holds a universe of wisdom, particularly in the context of teamwork and trust.